HISTORIC SPRINGS OF THE VIRGINIAS

A PICTORIAL HISTORY

ON THE VERANDA.

HISTORIC

SPRINGS OF THE VIRGINIAS

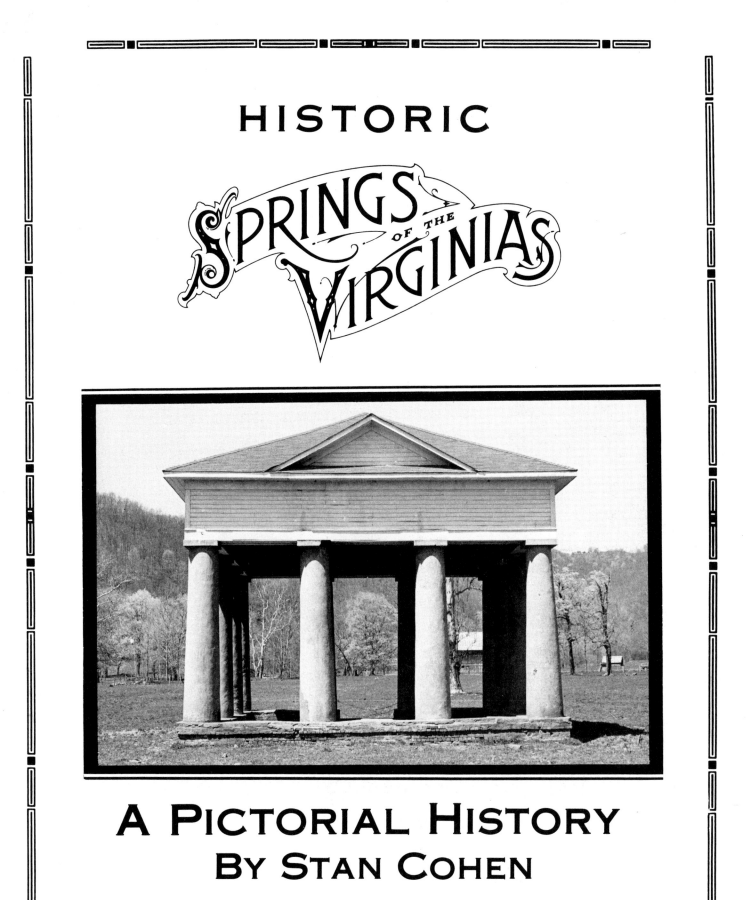

A PICTORIAL HISTORY
BY STAN COHEN

Pictorial Histories Publishing Company
Charleston, West Virginia

LIBRARY OF CONGRESS CATALOG
CARD NO.   81-80698

ISBN 0-933126-14-X

First Printing   May 1981
Second Printing   February 1983
Third Printing   March 1985
Fourth Printing   April 1987

Calligraphy by Heidi Hess
Typography by Arrow Graphics

Cover art work by
Monte Dolack and Mary Beth Percival

Back Cover Photographs

TOP-The "Old White" at White Sulphur Springs, West Virginia

MIDDLE LEFT-*Orkney Springs Hotel dining room in the 1960s, Orkney Springs, Virginia*
Gitchell's Studio, Harrisonburgh, Virginia

MIDDLE RIGHT-*Berkeley Springs State Park, West Virginia*   State of West Virginia

BOTTOM-*The Homestead, Hot Springs, Virginia*   Virginia Hot Springs Co.

PRINTED IN CANADA

PICTORIAL HISTORIES PUBLISHING COMPANY
4103 Virginia Ave. SE
Charleston, West Virginia 25304

Contents

Introduction

Researching the history of the many spas of the Virginias was like looking for lost pennies in high grass. The larger sites or the ones that are still open as resorts were no problem, but scores of smaller ones have simply disappeared, either physically, in the literature, or both. I spent many months criss-crosing the mountains and the lowlands following leads and my own instincts and believe that I have uncovered a great percentage of the spa sites. Still, there could always be one more behind that next hill or down that winding, dusty road.

The history of these springs, spas, resorts—call them what you may—is a fascinating tale. Although each story is unique, all the resorts were developed for two reasons—health and entertainment.

One can go back thousands of years and find evidence of people "taking the waters." The early Roman baths, especially at the Caracalla site in Rome, are world famous. Wherever the Romans went in their conquests, they sought out the mineral waters. All over Europe, springs were used and developed from the first days of human civilization. Names like Wiesbaden and Baden Baden in Germany; Aix la Chapelle in France; Bath, Brighton and Harrowgate in England and Spa in Belgium—which gave the world the name for these grand and glorious establishments—these names conjure up dreams of days gone by.

Some of the early American spas, established at the end of the eighteenth century, have existed in one form or another for more than 200 years. It is impossible to obtain an exact count of the number of springs that were actually developed into resorts in the two states, but 75 descriptions appear in this book. There are probably others that have passed into oblivion.

All of the resorts, both large and small, could be divided into three loose historical periods: Ante-bellum, from the late 1700s to 1861; post Civil War to World War I; and 1918 to the present. If one were to chart their development and popularity on a graph, the peak would occur in the middle 1800s, and the low point would be seen during and after the Civil War. The line would rise again in the late 1800s, but there would be a steady decline shown after World War I.

In Pollard's book, "The Virginia Tourist," he described the springs region of Virginia as commencing at Allegheny Springs, toward the south and west, and running north in a crescent to end in Bath County. He also called the area, "America's Sanitarium."

The springs region actually encompassed the entire length of the Appalachian Chain from New York to Alabama, but most of the resorts were concentrated in the Blue Ridge Mountains of Virginia and along the Allegheny Front in West Virginia. This book describes all the major springs/resorts in the two states and many that are outside Pollard's boundaries.

Most of the springs in the Blue Ridge region issue from the Oriskany sandstone and the Helderberg limestone (both of Devonian geologic age) at their outcrops on the limbs of anticlines (a geologic term for a broad upward fold of rock strata). The water which falls on the earth enters a permeable formation along the outcrop at a high elevation and permeates down through the strata to an outcrop at a lower elevation. The temperature of the water is normally a reflection of the earth's temperature. Thermal spring water comes from rather deep in the earth's crust.

The so-called mineral water, a phrase used in the early advertising of the resorts, is simply a natural water that has been impregnated with foreign substances to cause a decided taste or odor.

The classification of the waters can be broken down into six different categories: Saline waters have dissolved salts of calcium, magnesium and sodium. Berkeley Springs, like Seidlitz, Chillenham and Bath in Europe is a typical saline spa; Sulphur waters contain hydrogen sulfide and have a "rotten egg" smell. Sulphur Springs such as Aix la Chapelle and Harrowgate in Europe are like the White, Red and Salt Sulphur Springs in West Virginia. Chalybeate waters contain iron minerals. Tunbridge and Brighton in England and Sweet Chalybeate Springs are typical of such spas; In addition there are alkaline and calcic (lime) waters and thermal waters, with temperatures varying from 62-106 degrees fahrenheit. The resorts of Bath County are thermal springs.

The springs of the Virginias became famous, and the more fashionable and elaborate ones attracted visitors from foreign countries as well as from all parts of the United States. Some, whose clientele was composed mainly of wealthy and socially prominent people, were quite expensive. Others, equally desirable in many ways, and more desirable to some guests, were much less costly as well as less pretentious. There was variety in style as well as price reflected in the far-ranging differences between the elegant White Sulphur, Hot and Rockbridge Alum Springs at one extreme and the small community resorts at the other. People would come to these little spas to camp in cabins and sometimes even had to supply their own bedding and food.

The major resorts were founded on the premise that their waters, no matter what type, could cure common diseases at a time when medical science really could not do much for patients. Lured by the advertising, patients came and drank the water, bathed in it, or rubbed it on themselves, and the resorts prospered.

Whether the waters cured anyone is highly problematical, but certainly the elevation of the mountain resorts and the clean air helped many. The diseases commonly found then in low-lying areas were not found in the mountains. Just believing that the waters could cure disease probably was enough to produce an improvement in the condition of some patients. Things may not have changed much today. Consider the number of medicines and faith healers that abound and the places that people still go to be cured.

Two diseases prevalent in the United States then, yellow fever and cholera, probably were instrumental in the rapid growth of the health spas. Yellow fever had killed one-tenth of the population of Philadelphia in 1793, and in 1878 it claimed 5,000 lives in Memphis. Cholera had been known to kill 80 percent of its victims.

These two diseases did not exist in the mountains—cholera, because water, which carried the cholera vibrio, flowed away from the mountains, and yellow fever, because the mosquito carrier preferred the warmth of the seacoast and rivers to the coolness of the mountains.

Other diseases, too afflicted mankind at this time including: bronchial or throat diseases, hemorrhages of the lungs, tubercular consumption, pulmonary afflictions, dyspepsia, pheumonia, dysentery, skin diseases, diseases peculiar to females, gout, rheumatism, neuralgia, paralysis, diseases of the blood, disorders of the urinary organs and the list goes on and on....

This makes it easy to see why these sites became so popular, especially as there was little hope of being cured by other means.

If a person did not need a cure, there was always the attraction of social events and the chance to see and be seen. Those who could afford the time and money, travelled the circuit, going from one spa to another, in the summer months, and it was a delightful way to spend the summer.

The great prosperity of the Southern planter in the middle 1800s contributed to the development of the Virginia springs. The coolness of the higher elevations were a welcome relief to rich, lowland families from Virginia, North and South Carolina, Louisiana, Alabama, Mississippi and Georgia. They could afford to travel hundreds of miles to the resorts, but, with the great distances involved, it was only natural that they would stay for the entire summer, either at one resort or travelling the circuit within the two-state area.

Part of the objective, especially after the Civil War, was to be seen with the social elite. It was considered most desirable to stay at the same resort as the leaders of the former Confederacy. Robert E. Lee, spent considerable time at White Sulphur from the end of the war until his death in 1870. There was a lingering reverence for the old ways, particularly after the war when the old social structures were crumbling. Then, for a number of years after the war, the only people who could afford to travel long distances were Northerners.

Another important factor in the rapid development of the resorts was the phenomenal growth of the railroads as they expanded to the west. This made it much easier for people to reach the somewhat isolated mountain resorts. Those bound for the spas could ride the Atlantic, Mississippi and Ohio Railroad, the Shenandoah Valley Railroad and the Virginia and Tennessee Railroad before the Civil War. Afterward some of these were consolidated into the Norfolk and Western, Chesapeake and Ohio and the Virginian railroads.

If we may believe the glowing accounts that have come down to us, life at these old-time resorts was hardly a "rest cure" for invalids. For most of the guests, I suspect, health was only an excuse for going to a spa.

After reading about the activities and amusements available to guests, I wonder what kind of luck the resident physician had who prescribed this exacting schedule: "If the weather and other circumstances admit, rise about 6, throw your cloak on your shoulders, visit the Spring, take a small-sized tumbler of water, move about in a brisk walk; drink again at 7, and once more at half past 7; breakfast at 8. After breakfast, if you can command a carriage, take a drive, otherwise a slow ride on horse-back until 10. From 10 to 12, enjoy yourself in conversation or other mode most agreeable to you—*eat no luncheon*—at 12 take a glass of water, at 1 take another. From 12 to 1, take exercise at ten pins, quiots, billiards; dine at 2; amuse yourself in social intercourse until 5. Take a drive, ride, or walk, until 6—drink a glass of water; exercise until 7—take a cracker and a cup of black tea. If you are a dancer, you may enjoy it, but in moderation, until 9—quaff a glass of water from the Spring, and retire to your room." And, I wonder, how many patients followed the advice of the doctor who counseled against "deep potations of mint julap *(sic)* and other spiritous mixtures, after coming from the bath"?

There were many temptations to lure guests away from spartan health regimes. Almost every spa had a "fine band of music," billiard tables, pistol galleries, and ten-pin alleys. There were riding horses, buggies, and carriages for pleasure excursions. Day and night passed in a "round of eating, drinking, bathing, dancing and revelling." Gaming was much in evidence, and at some of the resorts horse racing was a daily amusement. Even those in the best of health must have found the schedule somewhat strenuous. Most everyone did go to the spring house three times daily for the prescribed tumbler of water, however. The spring house was one of the main features of every resort. They were invariably built in a circular or octagonal "Greek temple" style, and many are still intact today.

A number of factors contributed to the demise of the spas through the years. Three main reasons for the closure of most of them are: the destruction that happened during the Civil War and the changing social systems in the South after the war; better treatment and newly-discovered cures for diseases, especially after 1900; and, last, the start of the automobile age in the early 1900s which changed the fabric of American life. Cars gave people the mobility to travel from mountains to beaches or wherever else they wanted to go, and summering at the spas was no longer fashionable. A variety of other factors such as mismanagement, competition and transportation problems spelled the end for certain other spas.

And then there was one disaster that struck and often wiped out many resorts—fire. Some never reopened after the hotel or main buildings burned down, and many of those that did never regained their former glory. It appears that arson was the cause of many of these fires, a fact that undoubtedly reflects the fragile financial condition of a majority of the resorts.

I have tried to describe every spring site that had any kind of resort built around it. It is beyond the scope of this book to go into great detail about any of the spas, especially the large, well-known ones that already have an extensive written history. More information can be obtained at your local library with the help of the enclosed bibliography.

So sit back, read through the book and go back in time to an era when life was perhaps a little more carefree...

Dream a little...

Stan Cohen

Acknowledgements

This book project could not have been completed without the assistance of many people in both states. Dozens of people helped with ideas and suggestions and even with directions for finding some of the isolated springs, resorts and spas. While there are too many for me to be able to mention them individually, I would like to give credit to a number of people who took the time to help me with research or with securing photographs.

First, the staffs at the Virginia and West Virginia State Archives, Virginia Historical Society, Valentine Museum, Washington and Lee University, West Virginia University, Virginia Tech, the University of Virginia and various other county libraries and historical societies were most helpful.

Special thanks go to the following individuals for a great deal of assistance: Dr. Robert Conte for his help and hospitality at the Greenbrier Hotel; Dorothy Reinbold, librarian at the Waynesboro Public Library, whose interest in the old resorts is much admired; Fred Newbraugh, who has compiled a fantastic narrative and photographic history of Berkeley Springs; Dick and Tom Hambrick of Staunton, who were most helpful on sites in Augusta County, taking time from their busy schedules to assist me; Frank Holt of Staunton who provided the hospitality of his home and supplied some of the photographs used; Dan Jones and Carol Tuckwiller of the Roanoke Public Library, who were most helpful in my research; James Worth of Minnehaha Springs, a summer camp at the resort site where I spent three delightful summers as a youth; Harry Leake, who spent considerable time with me at Crockett Springs; Mrs. Erma McPeak of Eggleston, who provided photographs and the history of this forgotten spa; Shirley Henn and Gail Raiman-Helms of Hollins College in Roanoke, who provided considerable information on Botetourt Springs; Jan Wooton, director of the camp at Craig Healing Springs, who spent an afternoon showing me around; and Mrs. Robert Metheny of Warm Springs, who provided access to the many photographs of the Bath County Historical Society.

In addition, these people also provided much help: Alfred Gregory of St. David's Church, Va.; Mrs. Dan Burner of Woodstock, Va.; Ruth Lineweaner of the U.S. Forest Service in Harrisonburg, Va.; E.N. Lamb of Blue Ridge, Va.; Mrs. Ara Lee of the Fauquier County Library in Warrenton, Va.; Richard Scott Snyder of Stephenson, Va.; Wilmer Moomaw of Orkney Springs, Va.; William Wolfersberger of the Boy Scouts office in Winchester, Va.; Wilber Detamore of Staunton, Va.; Mrs. Charlsie Lester of Yellow Sulphur Springs, Va.; George Thomas of Glade Springs, Va.; William Gillespie of Charleston, W. Va. and a native of Webster Springs; Mrs. Mildred Claytor of Harrisonburg, Va.; and Mildred Miller of the Rockingham County Library in Harrisonburg.

The historic photographs came from a number of sources but primarily from the Virginia State Archives. These are indicated in the captions by "VA." The sources of other historic photographs are also noted. Most of the new photographs were taken by me in 1980. These are not acknowledged, but other new photographs are.

The quality of some of the historic photographs is not the best, but in most cases these were the only photos available. I have tried to research as many sources for photographs as possible, but in many cases probably no pictures were ever taken because of the remote location of some of the resorts and the fact that many were in existence only up to the Civil War. We are indebted to Edward Beyer, who published his *Album of Virginia* in 1857, and left us with an idealistic picture of the major resorts of the Virginias.

My one regret is that I was not able to get into Rockbridge Alum Springs to take new photographs. The site is owned by out-of-state interests and there was not time to make arrangements for a tour of one of the most elegant spas of Virginia.

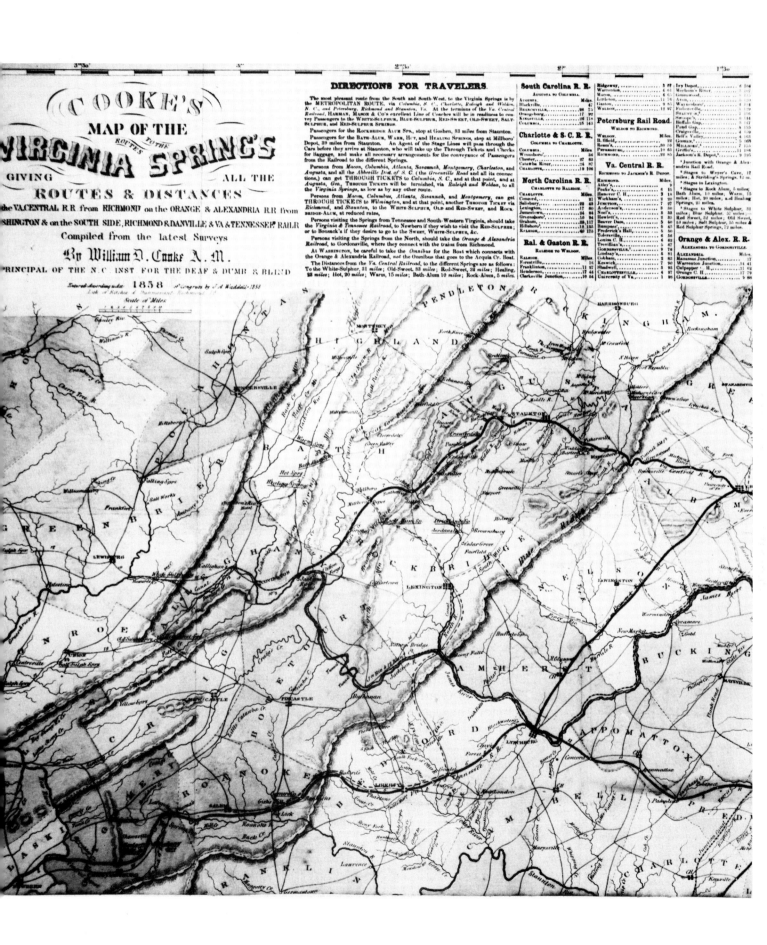

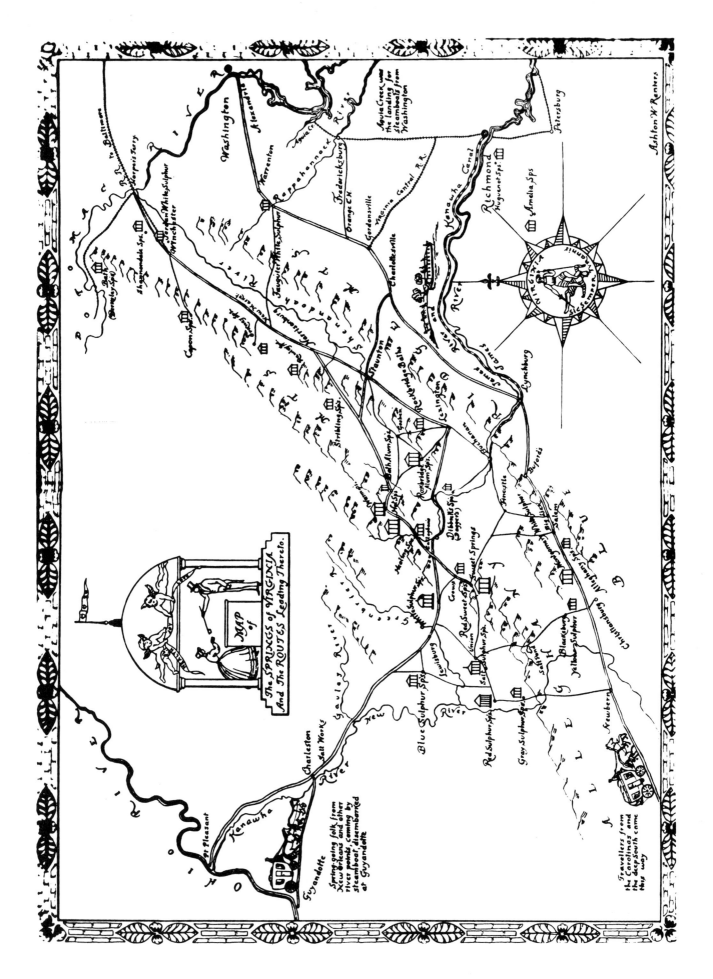

Virginia Springs

Different classes of people who frequent the springs from "Every Saturday" Magazine, October 29, 1870.

The Greenbrier

Allegheny Springs

Located four miles south of Shawsville on S.R. 637 off U.S. 460 in Montgomery County.

As one drives along the South Fork of the Roanoke River to the site of Allegheny Springs, it is hard to visualize where the buildings of the well-known resort used to stand. The site is now covered with new houses and large grass lawns. Only the well-maintained gazebo behind a house just off the highway gives one an indication of the opulence of the resort. Several other unpretentious cabins, a second gazebo in a private yard and the remnants of an old driveway with stone pillars on the west side of the highway are all that remain.

Not much is known of the resort's early history. The water was saline and reportedly contained nearly 30 elements. It became famous for its cure of the "American disease," dyspepsia. A hotel and 150 cottages built in the little valley and the foothills to the east were in use in the 1870s.

An 1874 brochure described accommodations for 1,000 patrons. Visitors could take the Virginia and Tennessee Railroad to Shawsville just a few miles north of the resort. Professor Kessnick's "Celebrated Brass and String Band" entertained on the lawn as well as the ballrooms. The facilities included billiard tables, bath rooms and a bowling alley. When visitors tired of indoor amusements, they could turn to walks, drives, hunting, fishing.

Dr. Isaac White, a well-known physician of the area, was in residence.

Dennis Whitlock's home fronting the highway is the one with the gazebo in the back yard. This large edifice was reportedly built by German immigrants in the *art nouveau* style in the 1890s. The central structure is made of cedar with decorations of gnarled twisted laurel branches and roots. Whitlock rebuilt the roof in the 1960s, and it stands as mute evidence of the resort's former glory.

Water was reportedly bottled at the resort until the 1920s. Apparently after World War II, the Sisson Brothers bought the property for $14,000 and subdivided it into building lots.

E.A. Pollard, in his book *The Virginia Tourist,* published in 1870, wrote vividly of the resort:

"The country around the Allegheny Springs is a succession of wild, strange pictures; and the astonished amphitheatre of mountains looks down upon the illuminated ball-room and scenes transported from city life. The advantage of these springs—an extraordinary one, when added to the surpassing virtue of the water—is the attraction of natural scenery just about them..."

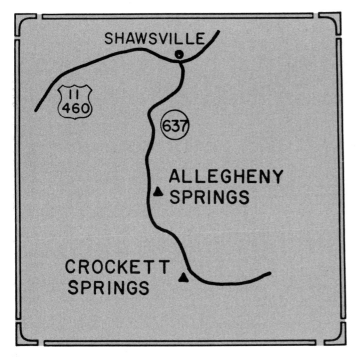

One of the original cottages at Allegheny Springs opposite the gazebo. It is now used as a weekend retreat.

Gazabo at Allegheny Springs. It is located behind the home of Mr. and Mrs. Dennis Whitlock, who rebuilt the roof in the 1960's.

FISHER'S VIEW—THE ALLEGHANY SPRINGS.

View of the Allegheny Springs from Pollard's book, The Virginia Tourist, *published in 1870.* VA

Amelia Springs

Located on C.R. 642, about three miles north of Jetersville, Amelia County.

The origin of the resort is obscure. The property was held by several members of the Willson family until the Civil War. It consisted of 685 acres, deeded to Frank Willson by his father in 1825. A few frame cottages were already standing and Willson built brick buildings and apartments in the form of a quadrangle. More than 20 frame buildings were also built.

The main building was a large brick colonial structure with a bar on the ground floor. The ballroom filled the front wing with a large fireplace at each end. Guest rooms made up the rest of the three story building.

On a hill overlooking the main building was a large two story brick dining hall which seated several hundred. A dutch oven was located in the rear of the hall.

The water was sulphurous, unusual for this part of the state. The resort achieved its greatest popularity during the period from 1843, when Thomas Clairborne Willson became the owner, until the Civil War.

One of the favorite events at the resort during this period was the Tournament of the Knights, somewhat akin to the English tournaments of medieval days. Also the local militia would have their muster day once a month at the resort and practice military drill.

Willson died in 1860 when he fell into the spring while cleaning it. The resort was sold to S.S. Cottrell in 1862 and was operated after the Civil War until 1877. It remained in the Cottrell family for almost 100 years until it was sold to the Chesapeake Corporation.

At the end of the Civil War, General Lee and the Army of North Virginia spent the night of April 5 at the resort before continuing their retreat to Appomattox.

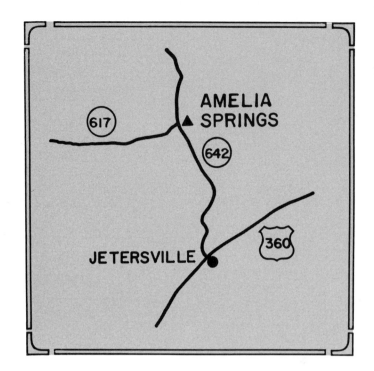

Augusta Springs

Located on S.R. 42, 3 1/2 miles south of Craigsville and southwest of Staunton, Augusta County.

A level overgrown field across from the Stillwater Mill at Augusta Springs on the west side of S.R. 42 is the location of this little-known resort.

A two-story hotel with an observation tower, a barn, chapel and employees' quarters were reportedly built. The remains of a bottling plant can be seen in the field, and the spring nearby issues at 750 gallons per minute. In 1904, $4 was the price of one case of 12 1 1/2-gallon bottles. A tall rock structure, which could have been a smokehouse, stands west of the old bottling plant. At one time a hunt club was established at the resort site.

The entire property is now owned by the U.S. Forest Service.

Remains of the bottling plant at the site of Augusta Springs.

Remains of a possible smokehouse at the site of Augusta Springs.

Basic City Lithia Springs

Located in Waynesboro, Augusta County. This small resort had its beginnings in Basic City, a development laid out as a manufacturing town in 1890 and consolidated with the city of Waynesboro in 1923. Basic City was named after the "Basic" process for steel making invented by Jacob Reese of Pittsburgh.

The Hotel Brandon, the central part of the resort, was designed by W.M. Poindexter, a famous Washington architect, and built in 1890. It sits on a slight hill above the city. It has a 260-foot colonnade and an observatory tower in Queen Anne style. The hotel has a terra cotta tint which makes it look quaint and old.

After serving as a hotel, it became the Brandon Institute and then the Fairfax Hall Junior College. It now houses the Academy for Staff Development for the Virginia Corrections System. The old hotel building and grounds are still in excellent condition and the Roman style pool on the grounds looks as if it would still invite bathers to take a plunge.

The stately old Hotel Brandon, built in 1890, now functions as the Academy for Staff Development for the Virginia Corrections System, but has not lost any of its grandeur.

The beautiful old Roman style pool just down the hill from the hotel is still in good condition.

Bath Alum Springs

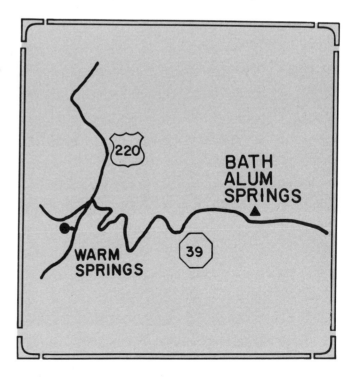

Located five miles east of Warm Springs, Bath County, on S.R. 39.

Bath Alum Springs dates from about 1740 when the first pioneers settled in what is now Bath County. As the name indicates the waters contain alum. Six springs were known, each with different properties. The resort enjoyed its greatest popularity when the pike beside it was the only entrance from the east to Hot and Warm Springs. But no village grew up around it, and the springs further to the west became much more popular.

By 1849, ten brick buildings had been built. The three-story main hotel had 98 large rooms, each with a fireplace. The pride of the building was its large ballroom. A smaller hotel was built on each side and several cottages radiated out from the hotels on each side.

Visitors would often take the baths at Warm

Springs to the west but stay overnight at Bath Alum. Washington, Jefferson, Madison and Monroe often stayed at Bath Alum and rode their horses over Warm Springs Mountain to the pools at Warm Springs.

Generals Robert E. Lee and Stonewall Jackson were frequent visitors to the springs. During the winter of 1861, the Bath County troops, under the command of Major W.H.F. Lee, son of General Lee, were quartered here. Confederate General Jubal Early billeted the remnants of his decimated cavalry here during the winter of 1864-65.

In 1878 the Grand Hotel could boast of rooms lighted with gas, electric bells in each room connecting it to the main office, hot and cold baths and, on each bed, wire-woven mattresses stuffed with hair.

In the late 1930s, all the brick buildings were torn down and the brick was used again to build the stately mansion and barn which can be seen from the highway today. All other traces of the spa except some large shade trees that lined the entrance driveway to the hotel have since disappeared.

The site today covers 840 acres, lying at an elevation of 2,200 feet and surrounded by beautiful tree-covered hills. Some years ago it was put up for sale as a possible new resort complex but today remains the home of only one family.

A view of the Bath Alum Springs hotels and cottages in the early 1900s. These buildings were torn down in the late 1930s and the same brick was used to build the present house and barn.   VA

A view of the Bath Alum Springs complex in Moorman's 1854 book of Virginia springs. Some of the original maple trees can still be seen along S.R. 39.   VA

The house built from the old brick as it appears today.

The barn built from the old brick as it appears today. The original hotel site was in this area.

Bear Lithia Springs

Located just off U.S. 340, one mile north of Elkton, Rockingham County.

Just off U.S. 340 to the west, down a small dirt road is a building that would spark the curiosity in anyone. Upon close examination it appears to be a cinder block structure covering an old spring. It was built in the past few years by the Coors Brewing Company, its present owner, to protect what was known as Bear Lithia Springs.

The area was first settled by Adam Miller who purchased the springs and 820 adjoining acres in 1741. In 1764, he sold the springs and 280 acres to his son-in-law, Jacob Bear.

It was a popular resort in its day, although no mention can be found of any elaborate hotel accommodations. A large circular stone wall was built around the springs many years ago. A special track was built in the late 1800s to connect the springs with the Norfolk and

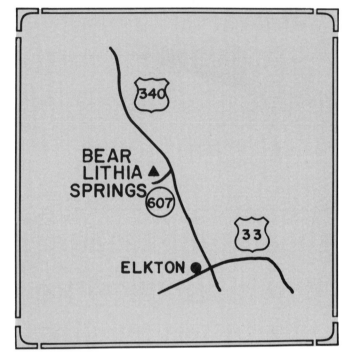

Bear Lithia Springs in 1918.   VA

Western tracks just to the west for the purpose of shipping the water bottled there. At one time, thousands of gallons per week were shipped out all over the world.

Today people can still fill up their bottles from the overflow. On the hill above the springs stands a brick house built before 1800, and just below the spring house are the remains of a chimney that was probably part of the resort complex.

The spring house over Bear Lithia Springs, built in the past few years by its present owner, the Coors Brewing Company. The brewery occasionally draws water from the spring.

Bedford Springs

Located four miles south of Lynchburg off of U.S. 460 near New London, Campbell County.

A ghost still stalks this ghostly place. It seems that after the Revolution a soldier returning home from Yorktown found his sweetheart wed to another. He left at nightfall, and in despair dismounted from his horse and lay down to die near the springs. A little girl from a neighboring farm saw his condition and in pity brought him a cup from Bedford Springs which revived him and restored his will to live. He never married, and it is said that periodically, at midnight, he is seen dismounting from a white horse and mingling, in a toast, his blessing to the spring water with a curse to his unfaithful love. He then disappears like a shadow with the wind.

Ghosts or not, Bedford Springs must have been an elegant spa in its time.

The property goes back to the 1750s and in 1836 a portion of it was sold to Peregrine Echols. He built a building which was used as a tavern. A deposit of alum was found there, which led to the discovery of a spring. No use was made of this discovery until John R. Maben bought the property, improved the grounds and built a hotel and cottages.

The resort was within four miles of the Virginia and Tennessee Railroad, and just south of the city of Lynchburg. The village of New London was encompassed by the new resort which was named Bedford Springs.

An 1878 brochure extolls the virtues of the resort. All the usual amusements were found there, it says, while mosquitoes and gnats were unknown. Apparently the resort even operated its own farm of 120 acres which surrounded it.

When the spa was discontinued as a health resort, a company was organized for the manufacture of salts from the water. The plant was located on the James River near Lynchburg. John Minor Botts Echols, son of the original owner, was associated with the business, but it did not remain in operation long.

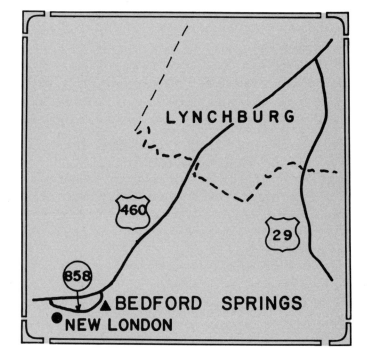

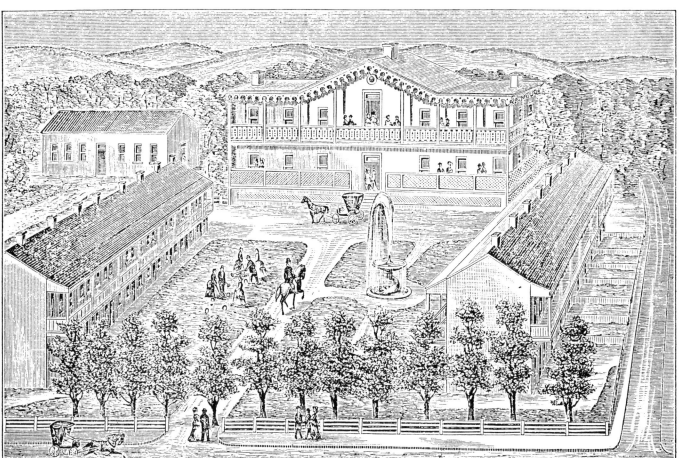

Bedford Springs Resort in 1878.   VA

Blue Ridge Springs

Located on C.R. 605 south of U.S. 460 about two miles from Blue Ridge, Botetourt County and 10 miles east of Roanoke.

Several of the major historic resorts in Virginia are so overgrown today that it is almost impossible to visualize the grandeur that was once there. Blue Ridge Springs is one such resort.

The history of the springs is connected with the Indian and game trail known as the Great Road which ran east-west through the area. The Indians knew of the supposedly beneficial effect of the waters, and they passed this on to the early white settlers.

Nothing was done with the springs until John R. McDaniels bought the place and built a small frame hotel in 1866. The hotel was built at a Virginia and Tennessee Railroad stop named Flukes, and the depot was incorporated into the structure. Subsequently, the more appropriate name of Blue Ridge Springs was given to it.

Guests could ride the railroad from many points in the South directly to the resort, but a spark from a wood burning engine touched off a fire in April 1871 that destroyed the hotel. Out of the ashes, the owner built a new and larger hotel, but the Panic of 1873 and the resulting debt incurred by the expansion dealt a severe blow to the resort.

In 1878, the company decided to sell the resort if it could get a good price. Then, changing direction, it decided instead to hire a Captain Phillip Brown to put the resort in the black. He had been manager of the Markham Exposition Hotel in Atlanta.

He immediately caused a turn around in the resort's fortunes. He advertised that the spring water was a great cure for the malady of the day, dyspepsia, and that the bottled water could be shipped anywhere in the country. Not only was he a very personable operator, but his advertisements extolled the grandeur of the mountain scenery, the purity of the air and the medicinal virtues of the water.

With help from the Norfolk and Western Railroad, which was connected to the resort in 1882, and the general upswing in business from the new chartered city of Roanoke, the outlook for the resort was vastly improved. In 1884, Captain Brown became sole owner for the price of $25,000.

The four story frame hotel along the railroad tracks had wide verandas with a covered bridge-walkway from the center of the second floor to the carriage road. A large fountain was built below the hotel, and the surrounding grounds were kept in immaculate condition. Brown built the Richmond Cottage with 32 rooms, the St. James Cottage with 24 rooms and the Lake Cottage in the 1800s. He elegantly furnished them with antiques.

With the resort becoming more popular in the late 1800s and early 1900s, many people rode out to the springs the few short miles from Roanoke in buggies, for an evening's

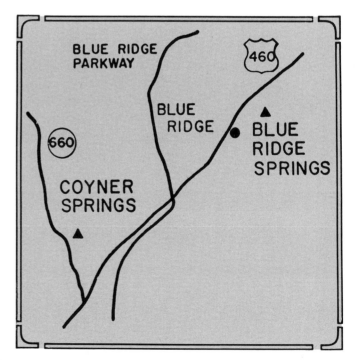

entertainment. Bridle paths were all over the mountains for the horse enthusiast.

Like so many other early resorts, the end of World War I, prohibition and the increased use of the automobile spelled doom for the once fashionable spas. Captain Brown died in 1912, and in 1915, Mr. Robert Augell, a well-known Roanoke investor, became the owner. He in turn sold out to the Jabbour Brothers in 1921. They made some modern improvements such as electric lights and a swimming pool.

But the world was changing fast. The springs, being so close to Roanoke, became a haven for clandestine love affairs and the quality of resort life and of guests decreased remarkably. The Depression virtually put an end to the business. Lake and Richmond cottages were torn down in the 1930s.

Mary Hastings, who was the proprietor in 1934, sub-leased the resort to a Major Robert C. Kent. Unable to make the resort pay, Kent, heavily in debt, returned it to her. However, in June 1934, Kent persuaded Mrs. Hastings to make a trip north with him to try to secure new financing. The couple was last seen together in Washington, D.C.

In July the body of a woman, later identified as that of Mrs. Hastings, was found, dead of gunshot wounds, near Stroudesville, Pennsylvania. Kent was arrested and tried at Fincastle, Virginia. He pleaded insanity and was sentenced to 13 years in the penitentiary, where he died in 1937.

The resort remained popular as a picnic-ground for church, private and business groups all through the '30s but on March 3, 1939 all the remaining buildings burned to the ground in a fire believed to be the work of arsonists. The property was eventually taken over by the Shenandoah Life Insurance Company which had held the resort as collateral against a loan.

Today, one can still see the remains of a spring house near Glade Greek but everything else was burned and has grown over. Many of the large trees that were conspicuous around the grounds can still be picked out above the undergrowth.

View of the covered bridge leading from the hotel and the large fountain.   VA

Blue Ridge Springs Hotel from Orchard Hill. It was built in 1866 and burned down in 1871.   VA

The grounds of Blue Ridge Springs.

The site of the resort is now a mass of trees and brush.

The only remaining structure is this spring house near Glade Creek. Water still issues from the spring.

Botetourt Springs

Located on the campus of Hollins College just off U.S. 11 on the northeast edge of Roanoke, Roanoke County.

It is hard to imagine a resort at what is today Hollins College, although the campus takes one back to the days of yesteryear. The history of the present-day college, founded in 1852 as Virginia's first college for women, goes back to the discovery of a sulphur spring in the creek bed on what is now the campus. This site was part of a 900-acre tract originally given to William Carvin as a royal grant from King George II in 1746.

Someone became aware of the curative properties of the water, dammed the stream and changed its course. The reputation of the spring began to spread.

About 1820, Charles Johnston obtained 475 acres and constructed a hotel at the spring site. He named it Botetourt Springs. The resort, including the hotel and cottages, pros-

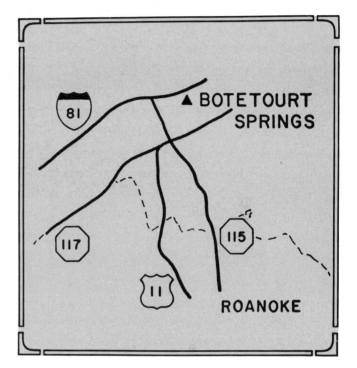

Front campus of Hollins College in 1891. The West Building is to the left.

Hollins College

pered immediately since it was conveniently located on the road leading from Washington to the south and west. Johnston placed an ad in the Richmond *Constitutional Wig* in 1825 stating that "the western mailstage from Richmond passing through Lynchburg will come directly to this place. Such gentlemen as do not wish to be encumbered with horses and carriages, can adopt that mode of conveyance."

After Johnston died in 1833, the resort's popularity started to deteriorate. The lands were sold off to permanent settlers until only 150 acres remained. The buildings were rented to various people who tried in vain to restore the glory of the old resort. Finally, in 1839, the resort closed for good.

Then in 1842 Valley Union Seminary, a coed school, was founded at the springs. Charles Lewis Cocke arrived in 1846 and re-established the school as a female college in 1852, and in 1855 it was named Hollins Institute for Mr. and Mrs. John Hollins who gave the school $5,000 to build the present East Building. In 1910 the name was changed to Hollins College.

The old, two-story hotel is incorporated into the present West Building. Wings were added in 1849, and the present building was rebuilt in 1900.

The springs as pictured on parlor screens.   Hollins College

-20-

The oldest structure on campus is William Carvin's spring house, located between the present West and Main buildings. It was built of limestone blocks and hand-hewn roof timbers in the late 1700s.

The present West Building was rebuilt in 1900. It incorporated the old hotel.

Buffalo Lithia Springs

Located on C.R. 732, just off U.S. 58, eight miles northeast of Clarksville, Mecklenburg County.

Of all the historic springs of the Virginias, this one was one of the most well-known because its bottled water was shipped around the world. It is located far from the majestic Blue Ridge where most of the famous springs were found and catered more to people from tidewater Virginia and North Carolina.

Colonel William Byrd discovered the springs way back in 1728. His Virginia-North Carolina border survey party was camped nearby on October 7, and they drank from the water. He wrote, "We had no other drink but what Adam drank in Paradise, though to our comfort we found the water excellent, by the help of which we perceived our appetites to mend, our slumbers to sweeten, the stream of life to run cool and peaceably in our veins, and if ever we dreamt of women, they were kind."

Ambrose Gregory in 1811 sold the 80-acre Buffalo Spring site to John Speed. It was a small resort consisting mainly of a tavern.

Speed sold out in 1839 to John Field and Alexander Jones and from then on the resort expanded rapidly. Existing buildings were renovated, cabins built, a large dining room constructed and a stage run was initiated to carry passengers the eight miles from Clarksville to the resort daily.

David Shelton bought an interest in the resort in 1845 and Dr. Silas Harris was named the manager. Facilities were constantly being expanded and upgraded. By 1849, Shelton became sole owner. He continued his ownership until 1863, when he sold out to Timothy Paxson of Maryland.

Until the outbreak of the Civil War, the resort was a favorite watering hole for people of southeast Virginia and areas to the south. The water was advertised to cure or help the following: diseases of pregnancy, scarlet fever, nervous disorders, chronic diarrhea, chronic cutaneous diseases, dropsical effusion, hepatic diseases, malarial cachexis and malarial poisoning. Many tournaments and balls were held through the years, and in 1858 hot air balloons were brought to the resort, causing much excitement.

In 1852 the resort was incorporated as a stock company and shares were offered for sale.

During the war, the springs remained open until the last year, 1865. The site was offered as a safe retreat from the battles but offered little comfort in the cold winter months, as it was designed as strictly a summer resort.

The springs did not open again until 1867 and during the next few years continued a slow return to normal. Paxon sold out to Colonel Thomas F. Goode, son of the one-time owner and developer of Hot Springs, in 1874. From then on, Buffalo Springs would become world famous and a household name in many areas of the world.

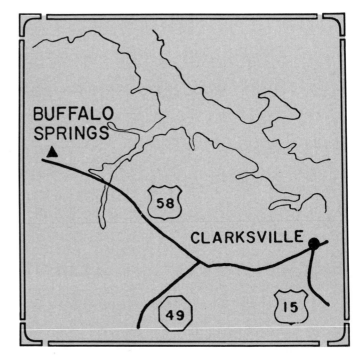

There were four springs at Buffalo, but an old neglected one, Spring No. 2 was developed and a bottling plant was built near it. The water was shipped all over the world. It was this spring water that made the resort famous and Goode a very rich man. It was the only spring there that contained lithia, a valuable ingredient in spring water. (The more common name of the resort was then Buffalo Lithia Springs.)

Goode believed that the water was all that one needed to drink on the premises, so liquor was banned. The resort was at the height of its popularity and most fashionable in the late 1800s. Goode built a golf course and baseball field, provided horseback riding, and even grew most of the food used on site. He died in 1905, and his wife inherited his interests.

Many stock companies were formed through the years to bottle the water, and the resort and bottling works continued to operate into the 1930s.

With the depression years and the decreased demand for bottled water, the resort was finally forced to close in the late '30s.

In 1947 the hotel was torn down and rebuilt on U.S. 58 as a restaurant and night club. Part of the property was inundated by Buggs Island Lake and only Spring No. 2 remains as a small park maintained by the Corps of Engineers.

A bottle of Buffalo Lithia Springs water that was shipped throughout the world.

Buffalo Springs Hotel before it was torn down and moved in 1947. VA

Burners (Seven Fountains) White Sulphur Springs

Located nine miles east of Woodstock, Shenandoah County, and one mile east of Detrick on C.R. 758 in the Fort Valley.

Powell's Fort Valley where Burner's resort was located is a long, narrow valley, 23 miles long by five miles wide, typical of the small valleys within the broad Shenandoah Valley of Virginia. It was used as a hunting ground by both Indians and white settlers. As it is somewhat isolated, it never received the population influx that other small valleys of the region received in the early 1800s.

Burner's, or Seven Fountains, has seven different springs, all within a half acre—chalybeate, magnesium, lithia, white, blue and black sulphur and limestone.

In 1850 a large three-story frame hotel was opened at the springs with a large ballroom and verandas that stretched the entire length of the facade. There were also detached cottages, pavillions and bathhouses and extensive gardens. Six hundred guests could be ac-

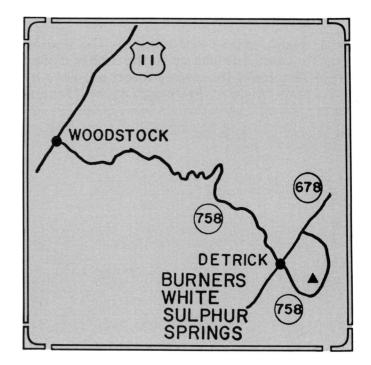

Beyer's rendering of the springs from his Album of Virginia, *1857.* VA

commodated. Three stage coaches ran here daily from Woodstock, Waterluck and Overall. A band met each stage as it pulled up in front of the hotel entrance. Much of the work at the resort was done by slaves.

In 1852, a notice in the Woodstock newspaper reported the sale of the resort for $12,000.

During the Civil War, Burner's was the headquarters of the famous Confederate guerilla leader, Col. Harry Gilmor. He was captured here in 1864, and Gen. Sheridan's troops burned down the hotel on his sweep through the Shenandoah Valley.

After the war, the resort never reopened but was used as a summer home by the Walton and Newman families up to the 1920s. Today the 400 acres of the former resort is owned by a corporation from Fairfax, Virginia. At one time a small fishing camp was operated here.

Remains of Burner's White Sulphur Springs in the early 1900's. The spring house in the center has been gone for many years.   Mr. and Mrs. Shipe
St. David's Church, Virginia

Remains of the spa as it looks today. All seven springs were located in this general area. The main hotel was located where the barn at the upper left is now.

Original pre-Civil War stone water trough leading from one of the springs.

Remains of the stone work around the springs that were covered by the spring house pictured on page 25.

Cold Sulphur Springs

Located two miles southwest of Goshen, Rockbridge County near the intersection of S.R. 39 and C.R. 780.

This is one of the many fairly large resorts that has almost disappeared, not only physically but from the archives of spa histories as well.

It apparently was a flourishing resort when a James Leech purchased it in 1858. Like most of the other resorts, it was probably inactive during the Civil War. A.S. Goode was the proprietor in 1869, and a hotel was reported to have been built in 1872 by Mr. J.B. Goodloe. In the summer of 1876 the resort was closed because of a typhoid fever epidemic in the mountains.

In the late 1800s, the resort was very popular with Staunton and Augusta people, and newspaper accounts report the hotel filled season after season.

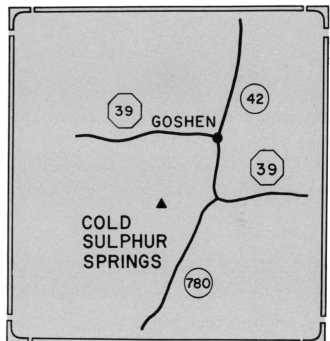

Overall view of Cold Sulphur Springs. This area is entirely overgrown with trees now.

Wilber Detamore
Staunton, Virginia

A new hotel was built in 1895 by Mr. J.B. Craig, reportedly 160 feet long. It burned to the ground along with several of the older cottages in April 1908. All remaining buildings were reportedly gone by the 1920s.

Today, part of the old resort is a campground and the remains of the spring house can still be seen about a mile up an old dirt road from the campground. Close to the spring house site, some foundation stones and a possible water well can still be found if one examines the ground carefully. Nothing else remains.

Spring house at Cold Sulphur Springs. Some ruins can still be found near this site.

Wilber Detamore
Staunton, Virginia

Remains of the enclosed spring can still be seen in a small clearing just off the dirt road about a mile from the modern campground.

Hotel site just off the dirt road near the modern campground. Some foundation stones and a possible water well can still be found on the ground.

Coyner Springs

Located on S.R. 660 just off U.S. 460 just inside the Botetourt County line eight miles east of Roanoke.

Coyner Springs has had many spellings— Coyner, Conner and Coiner. It was a white elephant to the city of Roanoke, but today it is the site of the Roanoke City Nursing Home and the Roanoke Juvenile Detention Home.

The history of the springs mirrors in part the history of the Roanoke area and dates back to 1770 when John Howard was granted 325 acres. In 1836 George Coiner acquired 165 acres of the original purchase. He died in 1843 and his wife retained 26 acres including the springs.

The springs had only local use until 1851 when Fleming James purchased the property and built a hotel and cottages. The Virginia and Tennessee Railroad was built near the resort shortly afterward and, to increase its business, the company built a station at the springs.

To attract more patrons, James dubbed the different springs: the White, the Blue, the Black and Chalybeate—thereby claiming for one resort the virtues ascribed to many.

In 1886, the resort was purchased by William Frye, whose son, Dr. William Frye, was an early Roanoke physician.

Life at the resort followed an established routine consisting of strolls to the various springs to drink the waters, croquet games, cards and dancing at night. The cottages were furnished with Spartan severity and the unpainted, unpapered, glaring white walls and ceilings were cheerless. There was a damp odor that seemed to permeate everything.

Along with Blue Ridge Springs, Coyner was patronized mainly by people from the Roanoke and the southwest Virginia areas.

By the time of the First World War, the hotel was in bad shape and was torn down. In the 1920s a New York man tried to revive the area but met with only slight success. Some years later the City of Roanoke came into possession of the property, and in 1939 the present nursing home was built as a tuberculosis sanitorium. The last tuberculosis patient was moved out in 1956 and the building stood empty until the City of Roanoke established the nursing home in 1958.

Today the old resort is peopled by senior citizens and juveniles who can look out over some magnificent scenery from its 124 acres of rolling hills.

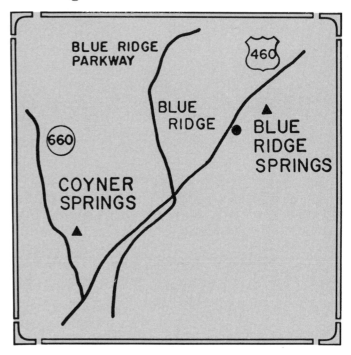

Roanoke City Nursing Home on the site of Coyner Springs. It was built as a tuberculosis sanitarium in 1939 and established as the nursing home in 1958.

Craig Healing Springs

Located on S.R. 658 12 miles southwest of New Castle, Craig County.

Although this area was first surveyed in the 1750s and the waters were probably discovered during this period, Craig County was too remote to produce any major development for more than a century. It took the building of a railroad to New Castle in the late 1890s to begin the development of this resort.

After the Civil War, two brothers, Eulis and John Jones, owned the site. It was known as the "Yellow Healing Springs." A post-war boom in resort development was in progress when Giles Smith of Allegheny County bought the springs in 1869. He was probably the first developer and he changed the name to Yellow Sulphur Springs, echoing the names of the near-by resorts of White and Red Sulphur Springs.

After 11 years, Smith sold out to John Sarver and Jeremiah Ross of Craig County who then sold the property in 1885 to a group of 11 investors. There was still no large scale development until these investors constructed the first substantial hotel building, possibly in the middle 1880s.

One of the investors, Martin Huffman, among the county's wealthiest landowners, bought out the others and promoted the resort mainly for its medicinal value. It was still far from the social gathering spot that similar spas in the mountain areas were.

With the entrance of Melville Ingalls upon the Craig County scene in the late 1890s, the fortune of the springs took a definite upswing. Ingalls was the president of the Chesapeake and Ohio Railroad and one of the principal investors in the resort. A spur line was built to New Castle to haul iron ore in 1897, and passenger service followed. Now people could take the train to within twelve miles of the isolated, low-key resort.

The potential iron ore boom in the area produced a series of real estate transactions involving the springs in the early 1900s, but the boom proved to be short-lived. The iron deposits turned out to be of such low grade that it was not feasible to mine the ore and haul it out.

By 1909, the resort was sold to a new company, the Craig Healing Springs Company. This move took the resort out of the hands of people speculating on land with iron ore deposits and placed it in those of people interested only in its potential as a resort.

The new company, owned mainly by investors from Clifton Forge, incorporated and started to make improvements. A new three-story hotel was built in 1912, called the "Merrimac" and later the "Jefferson."

Nathan S. Buck of Cincinnati, who supposedly was cured of a cancerous growth on his nose by the spring water, became a partner in the new company. Because of a disagreement with the other major partner, George Layman, however, Buck opened a new resort next to Craig and called it Monte Vista.

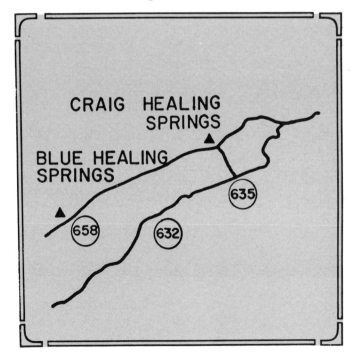

He built a hotel and cabins, a spring house and a bowling alley. In the 1920s a golf course was added and today the club house is still in use. In 1918, Buck died and both resorts were resold to P.J. Crowley of the West Virginia-Kanawha Company of Charleston, West Virginia.

After World War I, the resort really began to prosper and became the scene of many social gatherings and parties in the twenties.

The Florida land boom of the 1920s had a marked influence on the springs. A Florida group purchased the resort with the imaginative idea of persuading people to buy a summer home in the mountains and a winter home in Florida. Architects drew up a wonderous plan for a new resort complex with hotels, a lake and a spring house enclosure resembling a Greek temple. Some work was finished before the Depression ended all construction.

Resorts were closing all over the country during the 30s, but Craig Healing Springs fared better. J.W. Oulds of Lynchburg, who had managed to retain some of his wealth after the stock market crash of 1929, became the sole owner in 1935. He ran the resort in a very businesslike way considering the financial circumstances and made many improvements that are still in existence today.

Oulds and his heirs continued to operate the resort in the 1940s and 50s, but after World War II the business changed. With the additional expense of having to upgrade the sewage system, it was no longer feasible to continue the operation.

The Christian Churches (Disciples of Christ) of Virginia were looking for a site for a retreat and conference center and in 1960 bought Craig Healing Springs and the remains of the Monte Vista resort for $60,000. It is still maintained as a conference center, and the buildings and grounds are in excellent condition. The two largest hotel buildings were torn down in 1963 and 1971, but the old Central Hotel is still in use.

Old hotel at Craig Healing Springs, torn down in the 1960s.

Frank Holt
Staunton, Virginia

-32-

Craig Healing Springs Hotel dining room.

Frank Holt
Staunton, Virginia

A view of the main road in the resort complex in the 1930s. The building to the left has been replaced by the present brick building.

Roanoke Library

A gathering at the Springs in 1953. These buildings are still in use.   Roanoke Library

Present room and dining facilities. The buildings at the end of the street were used as stores in the heyday of the resort.

The Jefferson Hotel in 1952. It has since been demolished.

Interior of the dining room at the Springs in 1952.

Spring house covering the natural spring.

The old bowling alley of Craig Healing Springs now used as a storehouse.

Hotel foundations from the old Monte Vista Springs hotel built in the early 1900s above present Craig Healing Springs.

Spring house of Monte Vista Springs.

Crockett Springs

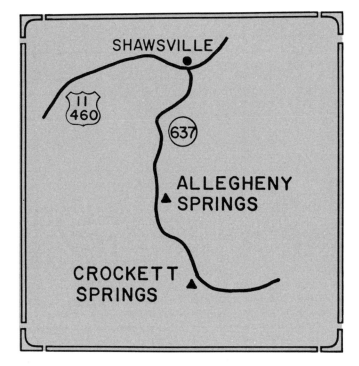

Located on S.R. 637, seven miles south of U.S. 480 at Shawsville and three miles south of Allegheny Springs, Montgomery County, on the South Fork of the Roanoke River.

This small spa just inside Montgomery County can boast of a beautiful setting surrounded by heavily forested mountains.

Legend has it that a sick Indian warrior, left to die by other braves who were retreating before the enemy, crawled to this spring and drank its waters. He recovered and later rejoined his tribe. He thought that the tribe's medicine man had cured him, but the medicine man thought otherwise. When he learned from the warrior about the mystery water from the mountains, he modified his practice, and took all the sick folk to the spring. There he performed his rites and made them drink the water. His patients got well, and his fame grew. Never was there a

A drawing from an old brochure of Crockett Arsenic-Lithia Springs.

Harry Leake, Jr.
Alta Mons

medicine man who could work such miracles!

True or not, the fact is that the waters had been known for many years, but no resort was built there until 1889 when the Crockett Springs Company bought the farm and springs from the Crockett family. A hotel was built, and guests could take the Norfolk and Western Railroad to Shawsville just a few miles away. The resort had all the amenities expected of resorts of the late 1800s. The water, which was said to improve the complexion of the ladies, was bottled and shipped around the country.

The resort, which was also knows as Crockett Arsenic-Lithia and Crockett Warm Springs, was in operation into the twentieth century. It is now owned by the Roanoke District of the United Methodist Church. The 700 acres is called Alta Mons and is operated as a year-round camp and retreat.

The hotel was torn down in 1966, and a parking lot now sits where the hotel used to. The old livery barn and one cottage, still in good condition, are all that remain.

The old Crockett Springs Hotel built in 1890 and demolished in 1966. Harry Leake, Jr.
Alta Mons

The site of the hotel is now the upper parking lot for Alta Mons Camp.

The livery barn is still standing near the site of the old hotel.

The last of the resort's cottages is now used for storage but is still in good condition.

Eggleston Springs

Located three miles west on S.R. 730 off U.S. 460 on New River in Eggleston, Giles County.

Eggleston Springs has known many names through the years—Gunpowder Springs, New River Sulphur Springs, Chapman's Springs and Hygeian Springs.

It was situated on the east bank of the New River opposite some magnificent geologic formations—towering, grotesque limestone cliffs.

Adam Harmon, one of the early settlers of the region, in 1849 was the first to build on the site, but he had no vision of using the spring water for commercial purposes. It was not until the early 1830s that any thought was given to establishing a resort here, and its first name—Hygeian Springs—was quite appropriate. Because of its highly sulphurous odor and taste it had been known also as Gunpowder Springs.

A Dr. Chapman took over management in 1853, and it was alternately called Chapman's Springs and New River White Sulphur Springs. He constructed a fairly large hotel in 1855, and the resort became a popular visiting spa for people from southwest Virginia and even as far away as South Carolina. The Virginia and Tennessee Railroad brought guests to Newbern in Pulaski County, and then a stage made the last 26 miles. Fishing in the New River became a favorite pastime of guests.

Unlike so many other resorts during the Civil War, the resort came through in good shape—but with no customers left. In 1867, Captain William Eggleston assumed control, and the spa was known as Eggleston Springs from then on. It was still hard to get to, but some guests discovered a relatively easy solution. From the railroad stop they could board boats for a leisurely 26-mile trip downriver to the spa. When the Norfolk and Western Railroad built a branch line along the New River to the West Virginia border in 1883, guests could take the train all the way and cross the river by ferry to the spa.

The old hotel was replaced by a new one in 1902. But because the Virginian Railroad moved into the New River Valley and its tracks came very close to the new resort, the hotel was moved further up the hill in 1906. With the coming of the new railroad, built mainly to haul coal from West Virginia to the Atlantic Coast, the peaceful and serene setting of the spa was spoiled and business dropped off through the years.

The resort ceased operations altogether in the late 1930s, and the hotel and remaining dance hall were torn down shortly afterward. Nothing remains today; new homes have been built on the old resort site.

The village of Eggleston, which grew up around the springs, is still somewhat isolated although a new bridge constructed in 1979 provides much better access to this scenic part of southwest Virginia.

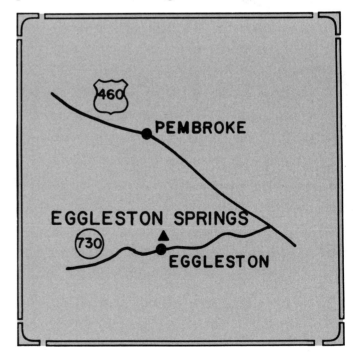

View of Eggleston Springs Resort in the 1920s showing the hotel built in 1902.

Virginia Tech Archives

The Eggleston Springs Hotel was built in 1902, moved farther up the hill in 1906 and torn down in the 1930s.

Virginia Tech Archives

A picnic at Eggleston Springs in 1923.

Mrs. Erma McPeak
Eggleston, Virginia

The original hotel at Eggleston Springs (then called New River White Sulphur Springs) was built in 1855 and torn down in 1902.

Mrs. Erma McPeak
Eggleston, Virginia

Fauquier White Sulphur Springs

Located on S.R. 802, 7.1 miles south of Warrenton, Fauquier County, off of U.S. 211.

Of all the Virginia resorts in existence before the Civil War, this was one of the most fashionable and elegant, with beautiful grounds and all the comforts possible for guests.

As far back as the seventeenth century this area was known to the Indians for its sulphur water. As early as 1717, a tract of land including the springs was granted to a Colonel Edward Barrow.

In the late 1700s, a Captain Hancock Lee built a lodge near the springs, the first of many buildings at what was to be known as Fauquier Springs (it was also known at various times as Warrenton Springs and Lee Springs). Lee had been an early explorer of Kentucky and found the spring water effective in treating his gout which he had contracted in his many years in the wilderness.

During the next few years the springs and surrounding area became very popular. Lee eventually sold the property to his son Hancock Lee, Jr. and his partner Thomas Green of Richmond, and they subsequently bought 3,000 acres of adjoining land on both sides of the Rappahannock River.

By the 1830s, Green and Lee, seeing the prospect of a major resort, built a large brick hotel, four stories high, 188 feet long, with a grand portico. It could accommodate up to 600 people and rivaled the prestigious resorts further west in the Blue Ridge Mountains.

The hotel was known at the "Pavillion" and 16 additional brick buildings were built in a semi-circle around it. A bath house, spring house and walkways were built and the grounds were splendidly planted and kept. At each end of the cottages three-story buildings called the Norfolk and Williamsburg Houses were built. Next to them were two two-story buildings, and to the north of the "Pavillion" the Warrenton House, which still remains, was constructed in 1830. In addition, 12 double cottages, each 56 feet long with individual porches, were built for invalids who could not climb stairs. One of these cabins is still in use today.

A bachelors quarters, "Rowdy Hall," was built next to the hotel and contained 70 rooms. Adjacent to Rowdy Hall were the stables and coach houses.

The present golf clubhouse is thought to be part of the stables. The spring, with a canopy still over it, is in the golf course area. Near the spring, the main bath house was built. It had a plunge bath surrounded by 14 private rooms. The usual amusements were featured at the resort—bowling, croquet, archery, billiards and musical entertainment.

A mile race track was built in the 1830s across the Rappahannock River. Medieval type tournaments were held on the flat lands with participants costumed.

Because the springs were relatively close to

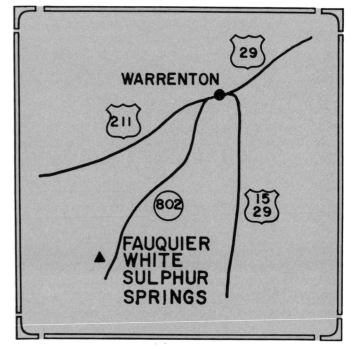

Washington, D.C., many famous people visited the area. Chief Justice John Marshall not only lived in Fauquier County but visited the springs often. Presidents James Monroe and James Madison had cottages there and Martin Van Buren stayed there in the summer of 1838. Henry Clay was a visitor along with Chief Justice Roger Taney, who moved to the resort the year he made his famous Dred Scott Decision (1857).

In 1849 the Virginia State Legislature convened in Richmond, but became panicky about the dreaded disease cholera and moved in June to the springs. Before making this decision, there was a strong feeling that the Legislature should re-convene at White Sulphur Springs, but the thought was abandoned when there was a report of the disease in the Kanawha Valley. The House of Delegates met in the grand ballroom and the Senate in "Rowdy Hall."

The Civil War had a profound effect on the resort. It was occupied by both armies since it was close to the Rappahannock. On Aug. 25, 1862, Union General Franz Sigel's artillery fired on the buildings, which were occupied by Confederate troops. A shell struck the Pavillion, and it burned to the ground. Another shell struck Norfolk House.

Like so many other resorts, Fauquier did not reopen after the war. Its buildings were in ruin; the social structure of the South had changed.

However, in 1878, the Fauquier White Sulphur Springs Company was chartered. A new hotel was built with 100 rooms, and part of the acreage was divided up into lots. Stock was sold at $50.00 a share, but the resort could not capture its former grandeur.

In 1895, the Bethel Military Academy bought the springs and hotel and moved in with 100 students. The hotel burned in 1901 and the school closed a few years later. Robert Winmill bought the resort in the 1920s, and eventually gave it to his daughter who in turn sold it to Walter Chryster, Jr. in 1943. It was again sold in 1953 to William DeForest Doeller.

Warrenton House was restored as a tavern, but today is a private residence. The former resort once again began to be used as a recreational area with the formation of the Fauquier Springs Country Club. No longer a retreat for people with health problems, the old resort is again a place for social gatherings, and club facilities include a golf course, swimming pool and tennis courts.

Beyer's rendering of Fauquier White Sulphur Springs in 1857, from his Album of Virginia. VA

Harpers Weekly in 1863 showed the Army of the Potomac encamped at the resort. Federal troops in 1862 fired on the Confederates who occupied the buildings and shells set many of the buildings on fire.   VA

DRINKING THE SULPHUR WATER.

GENERAL PATRICK'S HEAD-QUARTERS.

The hotel built at the springs in 1878 burned down in 1901.

The Warrenton House, now a private residence, was built in 1830 and is one of the three original remaining buildings of the old resort. It faces S.R. 802 at the entrance to the Fauquier Springs Country Club. Nearby is the restored Monroe Cottage.

The Fauquier Springs Country Club clubhouse was once part of the stables of the fashionable Fauquier White Sulphur Springs.

The spring house now sits on the edge of the golf course.

Healing Springs

Located on U.S. 220 2 1/2 miles south of Hot Springs, Bath County.

Of the three major health spas in the Warm Springs Valley, Healing Springs has been the least developed. It is believed that development began around 1850. Dr. William Burke, the noted proprietor of Red Sulphur Springs, noted in the early 1850s that the area was "as rude and wild as nature can make it" but later noted that a resort was being built.

There is no record of who developed the area or built the first hotel, but the Cottage Row, which was torn down in 1975, is said to have been built in 1856. The Healing Springs Hotel, today called the Cascades Inn, was used as a Confederate hospital during the Civil War. Later, in the early 1900s, the hotel became a fancy finishing school for young women.

There are actually two different springs in

Healing Springs, possibly in the 1850s. VA

the area—Healing and Little Healing—both thermal and having the same mineral consistency. In 1890, the Virginia Hot Springs Company came into control of the Hot, Warm and Healing Springs, and in 1895, Jakey Rubino, a trader on the New York Stock Exchange, bought the Little Healing Springs. As soon as he bought it he started marketing bottled water from "Rubino Healing Springs." The Hot Springs Company instigated litigation against him to stop him from using the word "healing" in his advertisements, as the water was determined to have no curative properties. Rubino finally won the case, but by that time bottled water was no longer popular with the public.

Rubino built a large, impressive house, and when the Hot Springs Company bought the property in 1923, the house became the Cascades Club. It is still used as a club house, for the championship golf course (Cascades) which was built in 1924.

During the early days of World War II, the ambassador from Vichy, France and his staff were interned in the Cascades Inn after they complained about their accommodations at Warm Springs.

The Hot Springs Company still owns the old resort, and guests who stay there can use all the facilities of the Homestead.

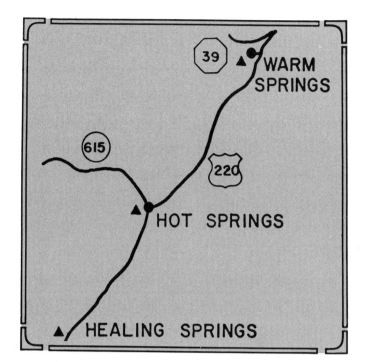

The Cascades Golf Club in the 1920s. The clubhouse was built in the late 1890s as the residence of Jakey Rubino. VA

Bottles of the Rubino Healing Springs bottling plant in the 1890s. This was actually Little Healing Springs just south of the Healing Springs.   Bath County Historical Society

Healing Springs in 1893. The dark building in the lower left is now the Cascades Inn. The cottages behind it were demolished in 1975.   Bath County Historical Society

Site of the Healing Springs just beyond the present Cascades Inn and Motor Lodge.

The Cascades Inn and Motor Lodge, the old Healing Springs Hotel.

Holston Springs

Located at the intersection of C.R. 614 and 714 on the North Fork of the Holston River, approximately three miles south of Gate City, Scott County.

Holston Springs, situated at the base of Clinch Mountain, was among the furthest west of the Virginia spas.

The springs contained four different types of water: limestone, chalybeate, thermal and sulphur.

No record could be found of when the resort was established, but it is known that the hotel was originally built as a women's college and was used as a hospital during the Civil War.

Fourteen Confederate soldiers are said to be buried across the road from the hotel site.

Rufus Ayres, a distinguished citizen and statesman from Scott County, bought the 2,500-acre resort in the 1870s and remodeled the 24-room hotel into his private dwelling. He built a large pond and maintained 20 acres as grounds. The house became the focal point for social events in the area until it burned down in 1914.

Today a modern house sits at the hotel site, and only the remains of the spring enclosure, a small stone structure and stately old trees remain to suggest the grandeur of days past.

Holston Springs before the Civil War. VA

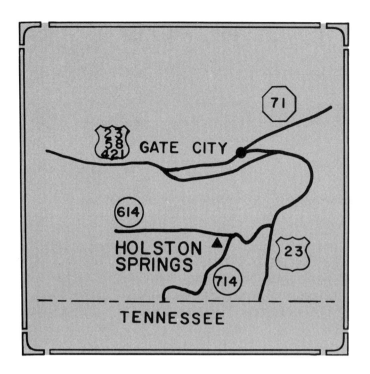

The hotel site is now occupied by a new home.

Remains of the spring enclosure at the old Holston Springs resort.

Hot Springs

Located on U.S. 220 five miles south of Warm Springs, Bath County.

One of the premier resorts of Virginia and the United States is in the beautiful Warm Springs Valley. It is the only Virginia spa still in operation as a public resort.

The three major springs of the Warm Springs Valley—the Warm, Hot and Healing—all now owned by Virginia Hot Springs Incorporated, have been visited for hundreds of years. An Indian brave discovered the hot springs in the 1600s, and by the middle 1700s a few white settlers had found their way to the valley.

George Washington visited here in 1755 while constructing forts for protection against the Indians. Thomas Bullitt built the first recorded inn here in 1766 because his home was being overrun by guests who were looking for a cure from the thermal waters.

From then until 1832 there is not much known history, but apparently there were several absentee owners.

Thomas Goode, a physician, acquired the property in 1832, and from then on Hot Springs has been one of the dominant resorts of Virginia. Goode was a good salesman; perhaps he could be called a medical huckster. He claimed that the waters of his spa would cure most diseases or relieve the symptoms. He expanded the resort and in 1846 opened a hotel called the Homestead—also the name of the first hotel—on the site of the present-day hotel by that name. He built cabins and bath houses, and many famous people made the trip to the Hot Springs spa as it became one of "the" spas on the summer circuit.

When Goode died in 1858, the hotel passed through many hands, and although it was still popular, it was not developed much more. Then came the Civil War. Both armies marched through the valley, and the hotel was used as a Confederate hospital. In spite of all these events, the buildings survived intact through the war years.

The modern history of the resort has its beginnings in 1890 when the South-Improvement Company bought all three spas in the Warm Springs Valley comprising about 4,700 acres. The company, part of syndicate headed by M.E. Ingalls, already owned the Chesapeake and Ohio Railroad.

The Ingalls family would be involved with the resort for years but in the beginning development of the project was turned over to Mr. Decatur Axtell, vice president of the railroad.

In 1892, a branch of the railroad was built from Covington to Hot Springs, thus allowing easy access to the resort. However, the hotel, built in 1846, was in disrepair, and it had to be rebuilt and refurbished.

At the same time the Virginia Hotel was built along with a railroad station—an idea borrowed from European hotel-stations. It was a magnificent structure, but built in the

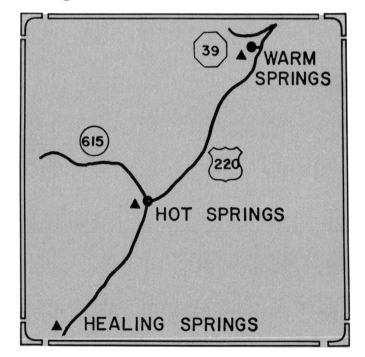

wrong place. It was at the lowest point in the valley with no view from the windows. The terrain made lawns and landscaping impossible, and the belching smoke from locomotives made occupancy less than pleasant. The Virginia was built as an all-weather hotel, and people flocked there in the spring and fall, but only until The Homestead was completed. The Virginia still stands, altered drastically, and has been a dormitory for resort employees for years.

By 1892 the present bath house was completed. It was modeled after the European spas and featured two main kinds of treatments—hot tubs for soaking and hot showers or "spouts."

The first golf course, consisting of six holes, was laid out in 1892. Seven years later, the Virginia Hot Springs Golf and Tennis Club was formed. Today golf is the main recreation at the resort.

On July 2, 1901 disaster struck the spa. A fire broke out in the bake shop, and the next day The Homestead and several outbuildings lay in ashes. The company started to rebuild immediately and by the spring of 1902, the main section of the present hotel, including a ballroom, was built, and by 1904 the west wing was completed. The hotel was truly elegant and one of the largest in the South

The Hot Springs resort as pictured by Beyer in his 1857 Album of Virginia. VA

when the east wing was completed in 1914.

The Ingalls family bought controlling interest in the Hot Springs Company in 1914 and took over direct management of the resort. With increased business after the first World War, it became necessary to add more rooms to the hotel, and the imposing tower that now dominates the building was built in 1929.

Even at the height of the Depression, the resort was the social gathering place for "America's elite." Mrs. Cornelius Vanderbilt's parties there were constantly in the social columns of newspapers. Due to financial problems caused by the Depression, the company was reorganized in 1938 and set on a solid financial support.

World War II saw many changes at The Homestead. On Dec. 20, 1941, Japanese diplomats were interned there until negotiations could be completed to exchange them for American diplomats in April 1942. This internment program proved to be a financial disaster for the spa. The Army and Navy both considered The Homestead as a possible hospital, but neither took an option on the building during the war years.

Then in May and June 1943, the International Food Conference was held here, and this attracted delegates from 44 countries.

After the war, the resort returned to the business of catering to guests. In 1948 the business was consolidated and the railroad was bought out. Holdings in the valley reached over 17,000 acres, including an airport, three health spas and farm lands. In 1959 snow machines brought skiing to the area, and this provided much needed winter business. In 1973, the south wing, with 190 guest rooms and a conference center, was constructed.

Today Virginia Hot Springs Inc. has over 700 guest rooms with a capacity of 1,100 people, operates two resorts, three championship golf courses, employs 1,000 in season and provides outstanding convention services and recreational facilities for people from all over the world. It is truly a world class resort.

The Hot Springs resort as drawn by Porte Crayon in 1857. The large hotel is The Homestead, built by Thomas Goode in 1846.   VA

The rebuilt Homestead that burned to the ground in 1901.   VA

The Virginia Hotel, a year after it was built. From a drawing in 1893.   VA

The Virginia Hotel was completed in 1892, and incorporated the spur line railroad station. It was considered really "swanky" for a few years, but lost favor after The Homestead was modernized. Its original cost was $112,000.

Bath County Historical Society

The Virginia Hotel as it appears today, greatly altered. It serves as an employee dormitory and shop area.

Virginia Hot Springs Company

LOBBY OF THE HOMESTEAD HOTEL.

Lobby of The Homestead taken in the early 1900s.

Bath County Historical Society

An invalid's chair used at the bath house between 1857-1890.

Bath County Historical Society

Panorama of the resort complex in 1892 showing The Homestead, Virginia Hotel, cottages and bath house.
Bath County Historical Society

The present Homestead rose from the ashes quickly in 1902. This view was taken about 1914 and shows the extensive buildings.
Bath County Historical Society

Interior of the bathhouse in the 1890s. VA

Servants on the steps of The Homestead sometime before 1900.

A wedding reception at Hot Springs in 1905.

The spa at The Homestead, built in 1892 and still offering full-line health treatment for the guests. It has been extensively remodeled. Virginia Hot Springs Company

The front entrance of The Homestead, Virginia's premier resort. Virginia Hot Springs Company

Magnesia Springs on the grounds of The Homestead.

A rear view of The Homestead showing some of the 19 tennis courts.   Virginia Hot Springs Company

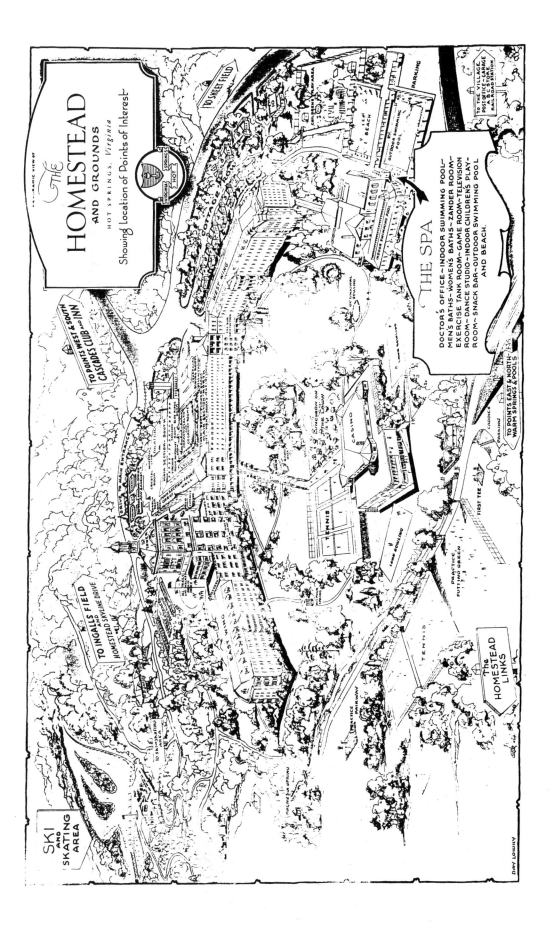

PANORAMIC VIEW OF

The HOMESTEAD

AND GROUNDS

HOT SPRINGS, *Virginia*

Showing Location of Points of Interest

THE SPA

DOCTOR'S OFFICE ~ INDOOR SWIMMING POOL ~
MEN'S BATHS ~ WOMEN'S BATHS ~ ZANDER ROOM ~
EXERCISE TANK ROOM ~ GAME ROOM ~ TELEVISION
ROOM ~ DANCE STUDIO ~ INDOOR CHILDREN'S PLAY-
ROOM ~ SNACK BAR ~ OUTDOOR SWIMMING POOL
AND BEACH.

SKI AND SKATING AREA

Huguenot Springs

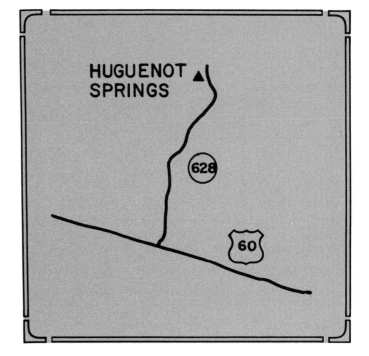

Located on Huguenot Springs Road, four miles off U.S. 60 and 17 miles west of Richmond in Powhatan County.

The medicinal qualities of the waters known as Huguenot Springs, originally called Howard's Springs, were known to the Indians long before the area was settled by white men. The springs were located on land granted by the British Crown to a group of Protestant refugees, known as Huguenots, who were driven from France in 1685.

In 1846 a group of men purchased a 95-acre tract that contained the springs and formed a corporation known as the Huguenot Springs Company. Before the spa opened on July 1, 1847, people from Richmond and the tidewater area who wanted to visit a spa had to make the long journey to the mountains of western Virginia. With the opening of Huguenot Springs, all they had to do was take

Huguenot Springs Hotel—built in 1847 and destroyed by fire in the 1880s.   VA

the Danville train to Robious and from there take a stagecoach for a one-dollar fare.

The accommodations included a three-story hotel for 150 guests and several cottages lining both sides of a spacious lawn. Three piazzas spanned the 150-foot facade of the hotel. The resort, which was well-known for its sulphur and chalybeate waters, became a center for social gatherings. The season closed each year with a riding tournament and a fancy dress ball, during which the "queen of love and beauty" was crowned.

Because it was so close to Richmond during the Civil War, the hotel was taken over as a convalescent hospital for Confederate troops. Local housewives served as nurses and attendants and brought bandages and gifts for the wounded. The dead were buried in 250 graves on a hill northwest of the site of the hotel. The United Daughters of the Confederacy dedicated a marker at the graveyard in 1915.

After the war, social activities quickly resumed, and many ex-Confederate officers took seats on the Board of Managers. But the hotel burned down in the 1880s. More and more people had been flocking to the seashore in the summer, and the resort's business quickly collapsed. Private residences took over the area.

Today the only trace of this once proud spa is the remains of the spring house located just off the main road in the thick brush. It would be very difficult to find without directions from local people.

The original spring house as it appeared in the 1930s. VA

Remains of the spring house can still be seen in the dense underbrush just off the Huguenot Springs Road.

Jordan White Sulphur Springs

Located on C.R. 664, the Jordan Springs road two miles southeast of Stephenson, Frederick County and six miles northeast of Winchester.

Many of the old spas are still used, but not necessarily as resorts. Jordan White Sulphur Springs is one such. It is now called Shalom et Benedictus and since 1973 has served as a state-funded home for youths.

The history of the area goes back several hundred years to the time when the Catawba Indians gathered there to perform dances and rituals and to drink the waters. When the days of the Indians were past, one Rezin Durall purchased the springs and hired a Dr. Williams to make use of their medicinal properties. Several cabins were built, and invalids came to find relief.

In 1834, Branch Jordan purchased the spa and erected a brick house and bath house and several cottages. The place became known as Jordan White Sulphur Springs. It is said that Jordan was a slave trader, and apparently he built cages in the old brick house to hold unruly slaves.

E.C. Jordan became the owner in 1867, refurnishing the houses and operating the resort until his death in 1889. His son expanded the business and erected the large brick hotel which is still standing. More than 300 guests could be accommodated in the building and cottages.

Jordan sold out to his brother-in-law, Harry Baker, a former mayor of Winchester, but by

Water from the springs was bottled and sold at one time.   Richard Scott Snyder
Shalom et Bendedictus

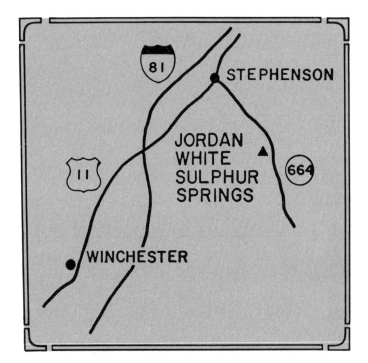

this time the patronage had fallen off to the point where the business was forced to close.

Later the resort was reopened and saw use as a private school for girls. From the 1950s to the 1970s it served as the Most Holy Trinity Monastery.

The old three-story hotel and one of the frame cottages is still in use. The large swimming pool has not been used in some years. The spring house, although in need of paint, still stands over the sulphur spring.

The spring house was featured in an early 1900s brochure.

The spring house today unchanged since it was built.

The old hotel at Jordan White Sulphur Springs, built in the 1890s, is in use today as a youth home.

One of the original frame cottages of the resort is used now as a staff house.

Massanetta Springs

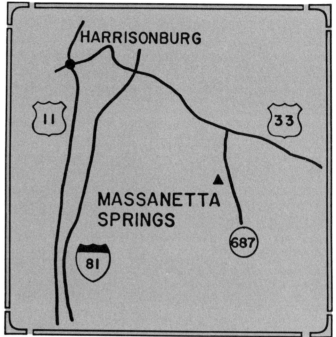

Located on C.R. 687, one mile south of U.S. 33 and 3 1/2 miles southeast of Harrisonburg, Rockingham County.

These springs were once known as Taylor Springs for Jonathan and William Taylor who purchased the property around 1814. In 1816 they granted the Methodist Episcopal Church a ten-year lease to use the area for spring and summer camp meetings.

When the Taylor brothers died in the 1830s the property changed hands several times, and much of its history has been lost. There must have been some structures at the springs during the Civil War, because a hospital is said to have been located there.

Dr. Burke Chrisman, president of a mineral water company, bought the springs in March 1888 and combined the names of Massanutten and Henrietta, the name of his wife, to establish

The main building and office of the conference center is housed in the old Massanetta Springs resort hotel built in 1909.

Massanetta Springs. He must have moved his bottling company here and shipped carbonated mineral water around the East. It was advertised as a cure for most of the ailments of the day. The water became so popular that people flocked to the springs and Chrisman built a small hotel to accommodate them. This building is still in existence and is known as Cottage A. It once faced the spring but since has been moved.

Dr. Chrisman died in 1909 and the small resort was sold at auction to Mr. J.R. Lupton. To attract guests, Lupton built the large brick hotel which is still in use today. Recreational facilities included tennis courts, an indoor bowling alley and small swimming pool. The grounds included 50 acres with a large stone structure built over the springs. Lupton met his guests at the Harrisonburg railroad station a few miles away and drove them to the resort in his Model T Ford.

After 1920 when the resort business declined considerably in many areas of Virginia, Lupton closed his operation and looked for some other use for the buildings. He deeded the resort to Hampden-Sydney College but their board of trustees felt it unsuitable for its use. In 1922 Massanetta Springs was deeded to the Presbyterian Synod of Virginia.

Through the years the resort has turned into a national bible conference center open to groups of all faiths. The beautiful campus encompasses 325 acres including a five-acre lake. Many improvements have been made through the years with the help of many denominational groups.

The spring house at Massanetta Springs. At one time it was surrounded by a metal railing from which hung tin dippers and cups.

Cottage A, the original hotel at Massanetta Springs was built in the 1880s. It has been moved from its original location but is still in use.

Montgomery White Sulphur Springs

Located on C.R. 641, just north of I-81 and five miles east of Blacksburg and Christiansburg and four miles northwest of Shawsville, Montgomery County.

Nestled in the east central part of Montgomery County is a small valley that once throbbed with the music, dancing and revelry of a major Virginia health spa—Montgomery White Sulphur Springs.

Its early history goes back to the middle 1700s when Col. James Patton received from King George a patent on 7,500 acres on the North Fork of the Roanoke River. The property changed hands several times until 1835 when James Kent bought the springs and 3,000 acres surrounding it.

In 1855 the resort was incorporated for $150,000, and this was probably the start of construction of the soon-to-be elegant resort. Since it was only two miles from the Big Tunnel on the Virginia and Tennessee Railroad, a station was built there and a small narrow

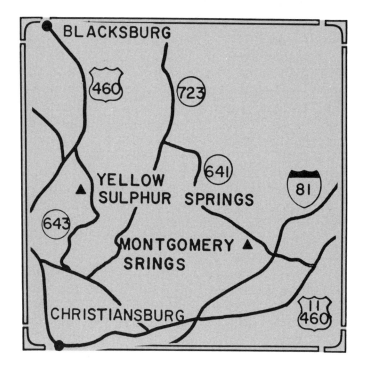

gauge railroad was constructed to the resort. The cars were pulled uphill by mules from the resort. There the mules were unhooked, guests were loaded into the cars, and the cars rolled back downhill to the resort.

Before the start of the Civil War, Montgomery gained its greatest fame. Twenty five buildings were scattered around the valley with extensive drives, tree-shaded walks and a great fountain in the center of the compound. The hotel and cottages could accommodate as many as 1,000 guests, and although the resort was not as elaborate as White Sulphur or Sweet Springs, it looked nice and was comfortable. Above the resort on the mountainside stood a geologic formation called the "Devil's Den" which had spawned numerous legends long before the resort was built. The "Devil's Armchair" was the valley in which the resort was located.

Beyers Album of Virginia *shows the Montgomery as a very elegant resort.*   VA

While the "devil" loomed above, people came to the new resort in droves in the 1850s seeking pleasure and health cures from the numerous sulphur waters. Some even came to fight duels under the oaks on the lawn.

In the early years of the Civil War, Jefferson Davis, president of the Confederacy met here with his cabinet and generals, taking advantage of the hospitality and relaxation of the area. Later the resort became a large hospital for wounded and sick Southern soldiers. Catholic nuns were brought from Richmond to nurse them. A smallpox epidemic hit here during the war, and hundreds of men died and were buried in the area.

After the war, the resort regained prominence and attracted many of the fallen Southern leaders. Gen. Jubal Early of the Confederate Army, the most prominent leader to return, was instrumental in 1873 in reorganizing the Southern Historical Society. Its purpose was to keep alive Southern traditions and the memory of the Confederacy. The Stonewall Brigade Association, was formed at the resort to raise funds for a monument to General Stonewall Jackson. Tournaments based on medieval practices, popular at spas before the war, were again staged by the Southern "gentlemen" of the day.

Business was thriving for a time, but the panic of 1893 spelled doom for Montgomery and many other resorts. James Crockett bought the resort and 457 acres in 1902 for $6,250 shortly before a flash flood forced over 500 guests to flee for their lives. Most of the buildings were ruined or damaged beyond repair, and this was nearly the final blow for the resort. A fire burned down the remaining structures sometime later, and the superstitious might say that all these calamities were the work of the "devil."

Today one can view the tranquil little valley and imagine both the pleasure and the pain that occurred there. In 1889 a monument was placed on the resort grounds honoring the fallen Confederate soldiers. In 1949, the owners of the old Devil's Den formation deeded to the United Daughters of the Confederacy a 20-square foot plot on the top of it. Part of the formation has since caved in, but the monument was placed there next to C.R. 641.

The Montgomery White Sulphur Springs Hotel in 1900. The resort was eventually destroyed by flood and fire in the early 1900s. Virginia Tech Archives

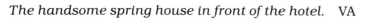

Gen. Jubal Early, a frequent visitor to the spa after the war and in 1873 the principal reorganizer there of the Southern Historical Society.

The handsome spring house in front of the hotel.   VA

A monument to the memory of the Confederate heroes stands along the road today, moved here from the valley bottom in 1949.

No trace can be found of the resort in the beautiful valley today.

Orkney Springs

Located on C.R. 263 12 miles west of Mount Jackson, Shenandoah County, off U.S. 11.

If all but one of the historic springs in Virginia were to be destroyed, I would hope that that one would be Orkney Springs. Its remaining buildings and its location at the foot of towering mountains make worthwhile the 12-mile drive up narrow, winding route 263 to the village of Orkney Springs and resort beyond at the end of the road.

This is a fairly new resort by Virginia standards, although the village at Orkney Springs was incorporated in the 1830s. Before the Revolutionary War, a Dr. John McDonald had acquired the springs and 360 acres, and by the end of the war there was so much traffic to the springs that the old Indian trail being used was made into a road. The farmers of the area erected rude cabins and tents in the summer.

The baths of Orkney have always been one of the principal attractions. The water is supplied from the Bear Wallow Spring opposite the main hotel, and there are seven other springs—the Sulphur, Healing, Arsenic, Iron-Sulphur, Chalybeate, Alum and Freestone. It used to be considered a cure for diseases, including mental and physical exhaustion and rheumatic or gouty afflictions, but the resort is no longer run as a health spa.

According to Miles Portlock Jr., who bought the resort in the early 1950s, Robert E. Lee's family owned Orkney before, during and after the Civil War. The Lee family apparently sold it around 1888. During the Civil War, General Lee's brother used the resort as a headquarters for his command while raiding the enemy in West Virginia. At one time General Lee's father borrowed $10,000 on the property and signed a legal document that touched off a court battle. It seems that the lending firm had Mr. Lee sign a deed instead of a mortgage, and the family went to court to have the deed voided.

The Maryland House, built about 1850, is the oldest building still standing at the spa. The once elegant Orkney Springs Hotel, the main building at the resort, was built in 1873. It is 100 by 265 feet and once had 175 bedrooms, a 40 by 155-foot dining room, a 50 by 100-foot ballroom, a reading room and billiard and pool rooms. Porches extended around each floor of the hotel, and each room opened onto the porch. Seven hundred fifty people could be accommodated at the resort in various buildings after Pennsylvania and Washington Houses and seven cottages were added to the already existing main hotel and Maryland House.

In 1884, Martin and H. Cabell Maddux leased the resort, possibly from the Lee family. The Orkney Springs Hotel and Improvement Company, with F.W. Evans as manager, emerged in 1890. The company built the largest swimming pool in the South, 90 by 50-feet, and this greatly added to the resort's attraction.

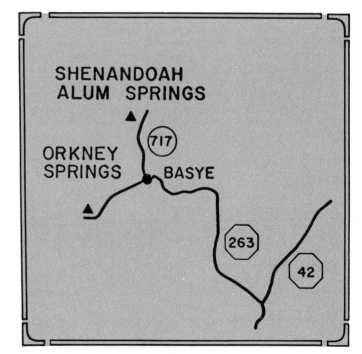

Entrance to the Orkney Springs resort at the edge of the village of the same name.

A second spring house, constructed about 1918 over the Bear Wallow Spring, the resort's main spring.

STEAM LAUNDRY.

BEAR WALLOW SPRING.

BATH HOUSE

DINING ROOM

A lithograph of Orkney Springs in 1888.

The resort operated into the 1950s. Then in 1960 the American Symphony Orchestra League, a national organization representing almost all the symphonies in the country, established its summer institute here. Each year the Shenandoah Valley Music Festival is held, and the old resort vibrates to the strains of music as it did in bygone days.

In the 1920s the Episcopal Diocese of Virginia had built a retreat called Shrine Mont next to the resort. In February 1979 it purchased the 950-acre Orkney Springs resort to protect itself from possible encroachment and to expand its retreat to accommodate larger groups.

The main hotel is being restored, while the first two floors are still in use. Other buildings and facilities are in good condition, and it would seem that in a few years Orkney Springs will represent a grandeur typical of resorts no longer in existence in the Blue Ridge Mountain area.

A string quartet plays on the lawn next to the Maryland House, the oldest building at the resort. It was constructed about 1850. There was once a very ornate foot bridge connecting it to the main hotel, but in 1951 a truck ran into it and toppled it.

Shenandoah Valley Music Festival
Woodstock, Virginia

The Conducting Fellows and orchestra musicians gather on the wide verandas at Orkney Springs Hotel to study scores, exchange notes on techniques and sometimes just to relax before the next rehearsal or performance.

Shenandoah Valley Music Festival
Woodstock, Virginia

The Orkney Springs Hotel (Virginia House), was constructed in 1873 and now is being restored by its new owner, the Episcopal Diocese of Virginia (Shrine Mont).

Pulaski Alum Springs

Located on C.R. 601, four miles off S.R. 100, eight miles north of Pulaski, Pulaski County.

This must have been a fairly large resort at one time from the photographs available, but it has sunk into oblivion. In 1859 the resort could house 100 people, and its waters resembled those of the Rockbridge Alum Springs. No record of when the hotel was built could be found, but it is known that it burned down in 1914.

The resort site is now the farm of C.E. Woodyard, and no remains are left. On the north side of C.R. 601, however, across from the farm, the old stone spring enclosure is still evident in the underbrush.

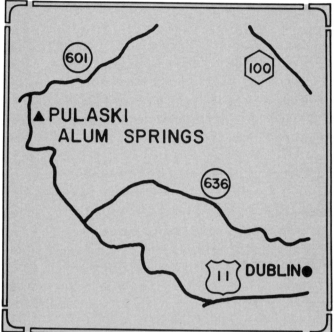

Pulaski Alum Springs resort in the early 1900s. The hotel burned down in 1914. VA

Bobby Woodyard is pointing to the remains of the spring enclosure next to C.R. 601.

The hotel site is now the farm of *C.E. Woodyard.*

Rawley Springs

Located on U.S. 33, 11 miles west of Harrisonburg, Rockingham County.

Of all the major resorts or health spas that have passed into oblivion in the past years, none would be harder to visualize than Rawley Springs. Without some direction one could not even find the site, which appears to have been partly on the side of a mountain.

The springs were known and used for medicinal purposes since 1800. In 1810 Benjamin Smith, of Charleston in western Virginia, built the first cabin for his mother who supposedly had an incurable disease. She recovered after spending the summer there, and as others followed, more cabins were built.

About 1825 the area apparently began to be called Rawley Springs for a farmer who lived nearby. Joesph Hicks was the first to promote the resort, but through the years many proprietors came and went. The greatest development occured after the Civil War.

In 1870 there were accommodations for 150 guests, but by 1880 this number had increased to 800. The old buildings had been torn down around 1875, but new building began and by 1885 a map of the resort showed extensive facilities including—the Washington, Virginia, and Baltimore houses, a bar room, a bottling house, bowling alleys, bath houses, cottages, a laundry, stables, an ice house, dining room and band stand. The three hotels were two or three stories high, with porches along the front of each story, and connected to each other by fancy arcades.

Rates of board in 1886 were $2.50 per day, $15 per week, $50 per month. Children under ten and colored servants were half rates and white servants were charged at rates according to the types of accommodations. There was a twenty-five percent discount to clergymen.

In June 1886 the Virginia and Washington Houses were destroyed by fire, and in 1892 one hotel and dining hall were rebuilt. The resort continued to function in one manner or another until 1915 when the main hotel again burned down. The other buildings either burned or were torn down later. The Massanetta Springs Company bought the area in 1914, but it never did anything with it.

Many summer houses and cottages now line both sides of Blacks (Gum) Run around the old resort area. Several stone foundations of the old buildings can still be found in the underbrush along with a stone spring house which was probably built at the end of the road after the resort ceased to operate.

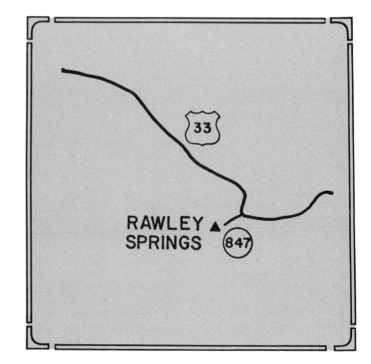

The Virginia Hotel at Rawley Springs around 1900. It burned down in 1886.

Spring house at the end of the road on the hillside above Blacks (Gum) Run. It was probably built sometime after 1915.

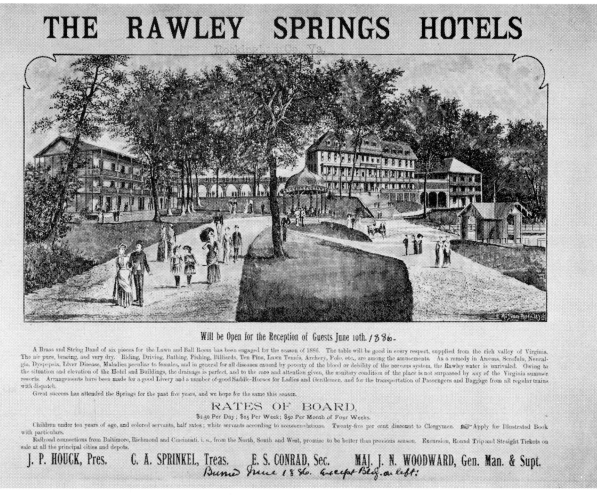

THE RAWLEY SPRINGS HOTELS

Rockingham Co., Va.

Will be Open for the Reception of Guests June 10th. 1886.

A Brass and String Band of six pieces for the Lawn and Ball Room has been engaged for the season of 1886. The table will be good in every respect, supplied from the rich valley of Virginia. The air pure, bracing, and very dry. Riding, Driving, Bathing, Fishing, Billiards, Ten Pins, Lawn Tennis, Archery, Polo, etc., are among the amusements. As a remedy in Anemia, Scrofula, Neuralgia, Dyspepsia, Liver Disease, Maladies peculiar to females, and in general for all diseases caused by poverty of the blood or debility of the nervous system, the Rawley water is unrivaled. Owing to the situation and elevation of the Hotel and Buildings, the drainage is perfect, and to the care and attention given, the sanitary condition of the place is not surpassed by any of the Virginia summer resorts. Arrangements have been made for a good Livery and a number of good Saddle-Horses for Ladies and Gentlemen, and for the transportation of Passengers and Baggage from all regular trains with dispatch.

Great success has attended the Springs for the past five years, and we hope for the same this season.

RATES OF BOARD,

$2.50 Per Day; $15 Per Week; $50 Per Month of Four Weeks.

Children under ten years of age, and colored servants, half rates; white servants according to accommodations. Twenty-five per cent discount to Clergymen. ☞ Apply for Illustrated Book with particulars.

Railroad connections from Baltimore, Richmond and Cincinnati, i. e., from the North, South and West, promise to be better than previous season. Excursion, Round Trip and Straight Tickets on sale at all the principal cities and depots.

J. P. HOUCK, Pres.   C. A. SPRINKEL, Treas.   E. S. CONRAD, Sec.   MAJ. J. N. WOODWARD, Gen. Man. & Supt.

Burns June 1886. except Bldg. on left.

The Rawley Springs Hotels in 1886.

Shenandoah Valley Herald
Woodstock, Virginia

-90-

Stone building foundations still found in the underbrush at the end of the road.

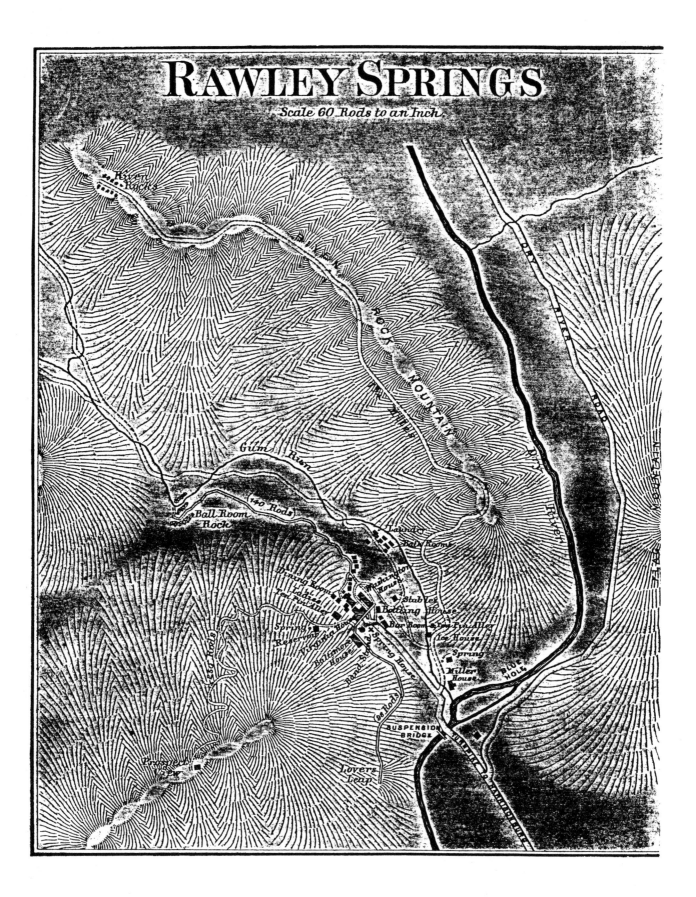

Rawley Springs from an 1885 atlas.

Roanoke Red Sulphur Springs

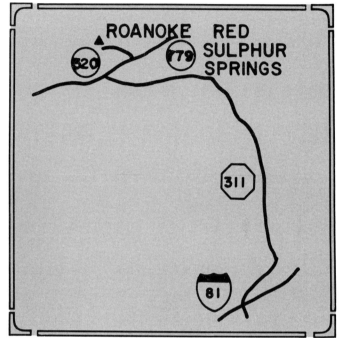

Located on S.R. 320 just of C.R. 779 and S.R. 311, ten miles north of Salem on the north border of Roanoke County.

With the construction of the Virginia and Tennessee Railroad in the 1850s, many isolated mineral springs became accessible. One was Roanoke Red Sulphur Springs which was established in 1857 by several men from Salem. They bought 700 acres containing a sulphur and limestone spring. The land was part of a mountainside that rose from the Catawba Valley, and fifty thousand dollars was invested to clear it, build roads and construct buildings. The resort opened in June 1858.

During and after the Civil War the resort was leased, and in 1879, Joe Chapman, a prominent hotel man from the area, leased it. He catered to people who wanted to escape to the mountains for the good, clean, healthful

Beyer's rendering of Roanoke Red Sulphur Springs, from his 1857 Album of Virginia, *must have been drawn at the time of its construction.* VA

air and the peace and quiet that this remote resort offered. Chapman later purchased the resort, and advertised his water as being valuable in the treatment of lung diseases. "Catawba Iron or All Healing" he called the water and shipped it around the country.

At the height of its popularity the main hotel accommodated 300 guests. Residents of Roanoke were repeat guests at the resort, and it continued to operate until 1908.

At that time, the State of Virginia, which had bought the resort in 1901, appropriated $40,000 to establish the first tuberculosis sanitorium in the state.

At first wooden pavillions were used for patients, but later more permanent facilities were built until finally the hospital building which is still standing was constructed.

The only evidence of the resort today is an ornate iron pavillion over one of the springs and an old two-story building above it.

Spring house from the Roanoke Red Sulphur Springs still standing on the grounds of the Catawba hospital facility.

An old building on the grounds of the Catawba hospital. The building could be part of the resort or one of the early buildings of the tuberculosis sanitorium.

Rockbridge Alum Springs

Located on C.R. 633, 1 1/2 miles west of C.R. 780, off of U.S. 60 and I-64, approximately 13 miles west of Lexington, Rockbridge County.

Tucked away in the isolated western part of Rockbridge County is the remains of a resort that some say was second only in fashion and elegance to White Sulphur Springs. It's Rockbridge Alum Springs.

In 1790 Alexander Campbell, the county surveyor, took an option on 2,000 acres which included the resort site. He took the option in the name of a friend, John Dunlap, because, as county surveyor, he could not at that time legally claim land under his own name.

The site was apparently not developed until Campbell's son James, started constructing buildings in the early 1830s in response to a growing interest in the alum waters. There were five alum and one chalybeate springs in the resort area. The alum water was touted as a cure for many diseases such as internal disorders, diarrhea, dysentery and skin ailments. It was bottled and shipped all over the country. Slave owners sent ailing slaves to work at the resort in the hope that the exchange of their labor for the "cure" would result in their being well by the fall season.

A post office was established in 1842 and construction continued, although a fire about 1840 had leveled most of the buildings. Before 1850 Campbell built what was to become known as the Central Hotel, a three-story building 30 by 360 feet. In 1850 the Campbell family sold out to Christian and Company.

In 1852, John and William Frazier bought the spa for $150,000, a large sum of money in those days. It was considered to be the most valuable single piece of real estate in the South. There were many buildings by this time—the Central Hotel, Virginia House, Vale House, Jefferson House, Gothic Hotel, Kentucky and Baltimore row of cottages, bath houses, bowling alleys, billiard room and, much later, a swimming pool and golf course.

By 1859, John Frazier's son, James, had become the sole owner of the spa which, by this time, was very well-known. It was the "in" place to go, especially for people from Tidewater Virginia. Quite a few northern people frequented the place, also.

J.J. Moorman in his 1859 book *The Virginia Springs*, stated that Rockbridge Alum "has appropriate buildings sufficient to accommodate 600 to 800 guests and new buildings are being added."

Frazier retained control of the resort for almost 50 years. During the Civil War, the resort, like many others, was used as a hospital. After the war, Frazier opened the spa again, but it was not like the old days.

The development of Jordan Alum Springs next door had a profound effect. From 1872 when the Jordan Alum Company was formed until 1880 there was bitter litigation between the two resorts. In 1873 the Jordan Alum

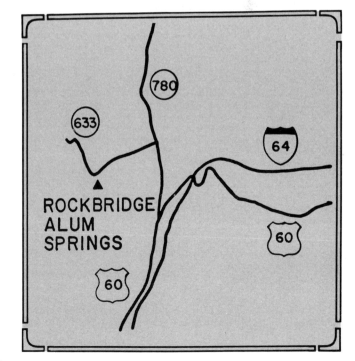

ROCKBRIDGE
ALUM
SPRINGS

Company erected a magnificent hotel, called the Grand. The two resorts merged in 1880 and the Grand Hotel became the focal point of the combined resort. For a brief few years this spa regained its former pre-war elegance.

In 1885 a narrow-gauge railroad was built from Goshen south to the resort. It connected with the C and O Railroad and provided good access to the resort. But in spite of this, the resort soon fell on hard times. Social conditions had changed drastically following the Civil War, and then by the early-to-mid 1900s the automobile had changed people's vacation habits, enabling them to travel to many places instead of having to spend so much time at one resort.

In 1902 the Grand Hotel closed and the resort sold at auction in 1909 for $18,000. Sinclair Lewis, the famous author, was a guest in 1918. During the 1920s the owners tried to promote the fading resort as a summer White House but to no avail. From 1909 to 1919 the Virginia Military Institute held a summer school at the springs, but the resort officially closed in 1919.

In January 1941, the Springs Corporation was liquidated, and the property, including 1,500 acres, was purchased by Bessie Patton and James Alexander for $7,000.

A few years later Mr. and Mrs. Harold Bailey bought the run-down spa to house their large collection of bird and animal specimens and rare books. Bailey was a retired naval architect who started collecting in 1889. On the site of the old Central Hotel he build a modern museum-library-research center and restored many of the old buildings, but he died in 1962 and Mrs. Bailey died in 1975 before they finished restoring the resort and establishing it as a scientific center. Heirs of the Bailey's now have the 2,000-acre former resort tied up in legal technicalities. It is closed to the public, but caretakers maintain the property.

Beyer's rendering of Rockbridge Alum Springs from his 1857 Album of Virginia. VA

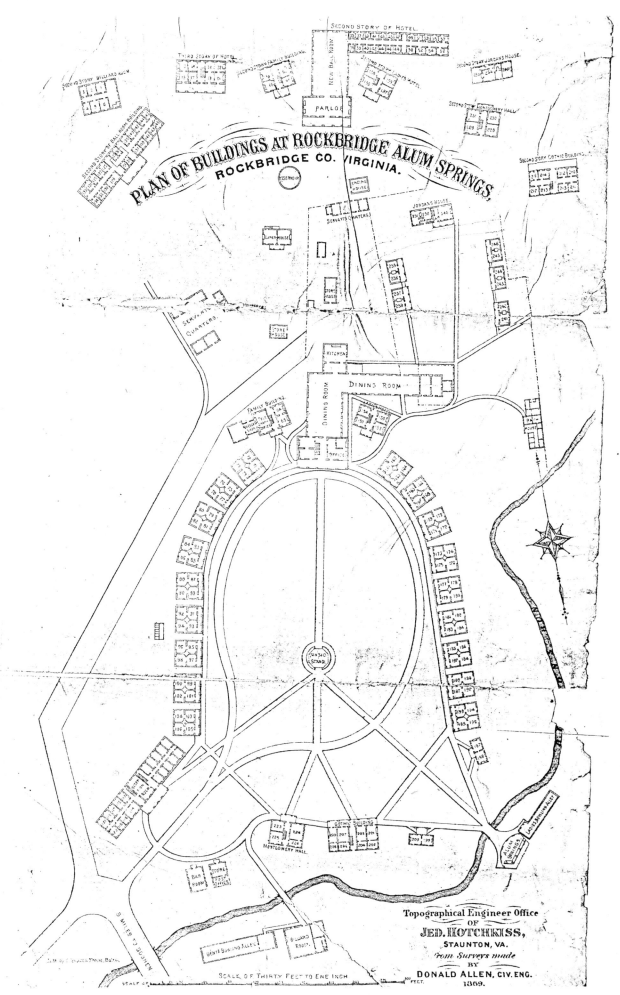

SECOND STORY BILLIARD ROOM

THIRD STORY OF HOTEL

SECOND STORY FAMILY BUILDING

SECOND STORY OF HOTEL

SECOND STORY LADIES HOTEL

SECOND STORY JORDAN'S HOUSE

NEW BALL ROOM

SECOND STORY OF BALL ROOM BUILDING

PLAN OF BUILDINGS AT ROCKBRIDGE ALUM SPRINGS,
ROCKBRIDGE CO. VIRGINIA.

RESERVOIR

PARLOR

ENGINE HOUSE

SECOND STORY MONTGOMERY HALL

SECOND STORY GOTHIC BUILDING

SERVANTS QUARTERS

JORDAN'S HOUSE

LINEN HOUSE

STORE HOUSE

SERVANTS QUARTERS

STORE HOUSE

KITCHEN

DINING ROOM

DINING ROOM

FAMILY BUILDING

OFFICE

BAND STAND

GOTHIC BUILDING

ALUM SPRINGS

LADIES BOWLING ALLEY

MONTGOMERY HALL

BAR ROOM

STORE

Topographical Engineer Office
OF
JED. HOTCHKISS,
STAUNTON, VA.
from Surveys made
BY
DONALD ALLEN, CIV. ENG.
1869.

5 MILES TO GOSHEN

GENTS BOWLING ALLEY

BILLIARD ROOM

SCALE OF THIRTY FEET TO ONE INCH

FEET.

-97-

The ornate spring house with its famous alum water.   VA

The Grand Hotel, built in 1873, was on Jordan Alum Springs property adjacent to the Rockbridge Alum before the two resorts merged. It was four-stories high, 175 by 125 feet and could accommodate 250 guests.   VA

A 1900 view of the theater, possibly in the Grand Hotel.   VA

The main entrance to the resort in 1912. The automobile eventually spelled doom for most resorts after the First World War.   VA

Montage of views at Rockbridge Alum Springs in 1912, seven years before it closed. VA

Rockbridge Alum Springs

═ INCORPORATED ═

THE KING AMONG MINERAL WATERS

ENDORSED BY THE HIGHEST MEDICAL AUTHORITIES

CONTENTS 64 OZS.

Medicinally: Use from two ounces to one half pint from four to six times a day. Always begin with a small quantity. Endorsed by eighty years' use, and the highest medical authorities of this and other countries.

SEND FOR PAMPHLET

IN 1883 the "Medical Association of Virginia" while in session at Rockbridge Alum Springs, *unanimously* passed the following resolution: "On motion, resolved, that we, the Medical Association of Virginia, do hereby bear testimony to our thorough examination into the medicinal properties of the Rockbridge Alum Water, and from our professional knowledge and information obtained, unhesitatingly endorse and recommend the same to persons afflicted with the following diseases—*i. e.,* some forms of dyspepsia or indigestion, scrofula, incipient consumption, chronic bronchitis, chronic laryngitis, chronic pneumonia, chronc diarrhœa, chronic dysentery, aphthous diseases, chronic skin diseases, torpid liver, and diseases peculiar to females.

In addition to the above, this water is endorsed by such high medical authority as Drs. T. Gaillard Thomas, Thomas A. Emmett, of New York; D. Hayes Agnew, of Philadelphia; Frank Donaldson, of Baltimore; Hunter McGuire, of Richmond, and Profs. Cabell and Davis, of the University of Virginia; Dr. J. S. Todd, Atlanta Medical College and many other distinguished physicians found in our pamphlet.

ROCKBRIDGE ALUM SPRINGS, INC.
ROCKBRIDGE ALUM SPRINGS,   **VIRGINIA**

ANALYSIS OF SPRINGS Nos. 1, 2, 3 and 4.
GRAINS OF ANHYDROUS CONSTITUENTS IN ONE GALLON OF 231 INCHES.

	No. 1	No. 2	No. 3	No. 4
Arsenic - - -	faint trace	trace	faint trace	trace
Antimony - - -	faint trace	trace	trace	trace
Lead Sulphate - -	trace	trace	trace	trace
Copper - - -	0.0424	0.04024	0.09287	0.10370
Iron Persulphate -	1.01850	1.94443	1.75922	2.90122
Manganese Sulphate	0.85955	0.09177	0.52511	1.37352
Nickel "	0.06298	0.14062	0.23969	0.22871
Cobalt "	0.03547	0.01432	0.08082	0.08124
Zinc "	0.11951	0.38906	0.20525	0.21748
Aluminium "	31.24652	42.60887	43.95506	72.37335
Calcium "	1.73110	3.22303	2.63598	2.31527
Magnesium "	0.88761	5.60586	6.37371	7.36110
Potassium "	0.17248	0.41290	0.38351	0.17586
Sodium "	0.02134	0.02743	0.02130	0.03463
Lithium "	0.01852	0.02006	0.02006	0.03241
Free Sulphuric Acid	3.23904	3.82512	2.04041	3.06633
Silicic Acid -	3.54627	3.69750	3.12807	4.38340
Sodium Chloride -	0.07547	0.10565	0.10565	0.14246
Calcium Phosphate -	0.01725	0.17251	0.20674	0.05174
Calcium Fluoride -	trace	trace	trace	trace
Ammonium Nitrate	trace	trace	trace	trace
Organic Matter	trace	trace	trace	trace
Total - - -	43.19155	62.35936	61.77342	94.83738

ROCKBRIDGE ALUM SPRINGS,
VIRGINIA.

These famous medicinal Springs having recently passed into the hands of a Joint-stock Company, it is proposed to place the water on the market at a price bringing it within the reach of the invalid public.

For more than half a century it has grown steadily in repute as a Medicinal Agent in a wide range of Chronic diseases, and prior to the late war it had attained a fame unapproached by any other mineral water in this country.

It first attained celebrity by its complete and unquestionable cure of *Scrofula* in its worst and most aggravated forms. Cutaneous Eruptive Diseases yielded to its action, and soon *Chronic Diarrhœa* and *Dysentery* were added to the list of its conquests. The powerful *alterative* effects of the water early attracted the notice of the profession, and many of its most distinguished members have certified to its efficacy in a great variety of depraved conditions of the system, as *Torpid Liver, Hemorrhage from the Kidneys, Hemorrhoids, Chronic Bronchitis, Catarrh of the Throat and Nasal Passages, Lesions of the Mucous Membrane generally.* Multitudes of women can testify to its unsurpassed efficacy in the relief and cure of those ailments peculiar to their sex. The fine tonic properties of the water give it great potency in all *anæmic* conditions of the system, invigorating the appetite and increasing and enriching the blood. It has repeatedly proven its efficacy in *Diabetes Mellitus*, speedily correcting the saccharine depravity of the urine and restoring the wasted flesh and strength of the patient. Probably in no type of disease has its efficacy been better attested or more unfailing than in *Dyspepsia* in its varied and most distressing forms.

We have from under their hands written statements verifying all, and much more than all we have here said, from such acknowledged authorities in medicine as Drs. Cabell and Davis, University of Va.; J. Gaillard Thomas and Thos. Aldis Emmet, New York; Stone and Cartwright, New Orleans. The last named having broken in health and lost his hearing by his exposure and labors in Natchez in the first invasion of Asiatic Cholera in this country, spent two years abroad in visiting and studying the most noted spas of Europe. On his return to this country he spent his first summer at the Rockbridge Alum Springs, and ever after, as long as he lived, he continued to send his patients of the Southern country to these Springs, and to order or prescribe the water for them. In a letter addressed by him to the former proprietor, Mr. Wm. Frazier, bearing date "New Orleans, July 28, 1855," after an elaborate comparison of this water, both in its constituent elements and its observed effects, with nearly all the most celebrated mineral waters of Europe, he concluded in these words: "In truth I know of no waters in Europe or America so rich in medical substances as that of your Rockbridge Springs."

To the list of medical names above printed, we might add a score of other distinguished physicians whose statements will be found in our Springs pamphlet.

This water will be sold in Cases of one dozen half-gallon bottles, delivered on the cars of the C. & O. Railway at Goshen, at $5.00 per case, and will shortly be placed with leading Druggists of the U. S. and Canada.

A DELIGHTFUL SUMMER RESORT.

This Company having lately bought the contiguous property called the "Jordan Alum Springs," have consolidated the two in one establishment, to be known as "The Rockbridge Alum Springs," and have placed the whole under the management of

Mr. Wm. Frazier,

who was for many years, down to 1869, proprietor and manager of the original Alum Springs.

They have elected Prof. J. Staige Davis, of the University of Virginia, *Resident Physician*.

They have fitted up the entire premises in the most complete style, and will open it hereafter to the public on June 1st of each year.

All the usual attractions and diversions are provided for—Choice Band and Ball-room Music, Billiards, Bowling, and excellent Livery, &c., &c.

In short, no effort will be spared to make this one of the most agreeable, as nature has made it one of the most healthful, resorts in the two Virginias.

J. Fred. Effinger, President,

Rockbridge Alum Springs Co.

280½

Rockbridge Baths

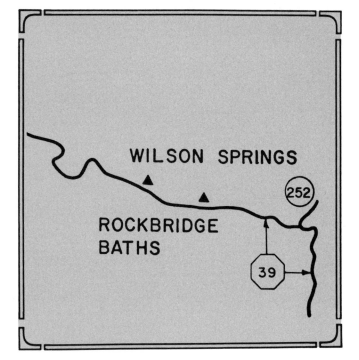

Located on S.R. 39 midway between Lexington and Goshen, Rockbridge County, at the village of Rockbridge Baths.

This small community was called Rockbridge Baths for the first time in 1857. Earlier it had been known as Jordan's Spring. A hotel was built in 1857 at the time of the incorporation of the Rockbridge Baths Company.

After the Civil War, General Robert E. Lee was sometimes a guest at the resort. He wrote to his wife from Rockbridge in September 1865: "On the morning of the 22nd, I rode over here...I have taken the baths every day since my arrival, and like them very much. In fact they are delightful, and I wish you were all here to enjoy them."

In 1874, Dr. Samuel Brown Morrison, who had been a doctor in the Confederate Army, rented the hotel and for the next 26 years operated it as a sanitarium. Dr. Morrison's ra-

Rockbridge Baths Hotel, Cottage Row South.

Frank Holt
Staunton, Virginia

diant personality and his skill as a physician made the place very popular with people who were looking for something other than gaiety and amusement.

There were two bathing pools filled by a number of springs bubbling up from the bottom. The water temperature was a constant 72°, which was delightfully cool on a hot summer day.

Because of illness, Dr. Morrison had to give up the resort in 1900, and a succession of owners followed him. But when Dr. Morrison left, so did most of the patrons. In 1921 the Virginia Military Institute took over the property and established a summer school. In 1926 the hotel burned to the ground and was never rebuilt. VMI then sold the property and closed the summer school, but the swimming pool, part of the dance hall and some cottages can still be seen.

The old structure enclosing the "baths"—actually a pool of warm water fed by multiple springs—is still standing in the village along S.R. 39.

Maury General Store at Rockbridge Baths. The right side of this building was part of the dance hall at the resort.

Rock Enon Springs

Located on C.R. 683 off of C.R. 704 and U.S. 50 18 miles west of Winchester, Frederick County.

This old resort, now owned by the Shenandoah Area Council of the Boy Scouts of America, was once known as Capper Springs. There are six mineral springs: iron, sulphur, lithia, limestone, Capper Healing Water and a large spring on the slope of North Mountain that supplied the hotel with running water.

This is another resort that was located in Lord Fairfax's land grant. According to legend, John Capper, the first white settler in the region, built a cabin near the resort site.

There were many different owners until in 1856 William Marker bought 42 acres including five containing the springs. He built the first hotel and developed the area as a summer resort. In 1859 a post office was established there with Marker as postmaster. He also formed a partnership with Mahlon Gore to further the development of the resort.

The resort had several subsequent owners until it was bought in 1873 by the Rock Enon Springs Company. The company made extensive improvements. It built an addition to Marker's original hotel, bringing the number of rooms to 450 and added a large ballroom and dining room. The company also built additional cottages, a bowling alley, billiard room, a band pavillion and bath houses. It constructed an observation tower on a ridge west of the hotel.

For 44 years, from 1875 to 1919, the resort

Rock Enon Springs resort as it looked in 1883. VA

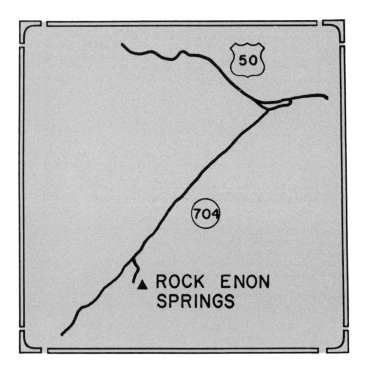

was owned and operated by Adam Pratt, who added many acres of land through the years. He did not approve of alcohol and did not allow any at the resort. In 1919 Pratt and his sons sold the entire resort to Fred Glaize and Lee Herrell after which several of the buildings and the original wing of the hotel were torn down.

The post office was discontinued in 1924, and the remainder of the hotel was torn down in 1942. In 1945 Mr. Glaize conveyed 570 acres including the old resort to the Boy Scouts, and it has been used as a summer camp since then.

The large 450 room hotel at Rock Enon Springs in 1918. The first part was built in 1856; the enlarged hotel was completely torn down in 1942.

William Wolfersberger
Winchester, Virginia

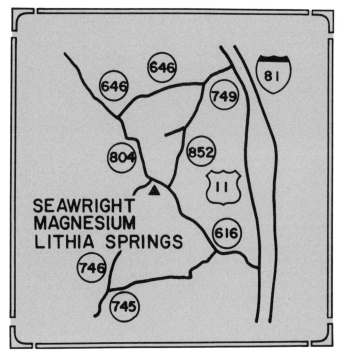

Located at the junction of C.R. 804 and 746, three miles west of U.S. 11, 10 miles north of Staunton, Augusta County.

These springs were known in the beginning of the 19th Century, but the knowledge seems to have been lost until 1876 when the site was rediscovered, according to a local newspaper. In 1890, Capt.E.L. Edmondson of Staunton purchased the springs and operated a business until at least 1909. He started bottling the water and shipping it around the country. The water is still bottled and the bottling plant at the springs is in excellent condition.

Another newspaper account from 1898 states that the Seawright Magnesian Lithia Company was organized in that year. After 1900 the company decided to build a sanitarium at the site and authorized a $15,000 bond issue. This bond was retired, and in 1908 a $30,000 bond was authorized and issued to build a large hotel.

The three-story hotel, although only partially completed, was opened for advertising purposes during the summer of 1908. It was on a hill overlooking the springs. By the spring of 1909 the hotel was finished except for the installation of a heating system, and completely booked, it was scheduled to open on June 28, 1909. This was not to be however. The hotel burned to the ground on July 17 in a fire thought to have been set by an arsonist. Thus it had the shortest life of any of the Virginia hotels.

The hotel was never rebuilt, but a swimming pool was added and the the spring was covered. The area is now privately owned. The swimming pool is being filled in and the bottling plant sits dormant.

The spring at Seawright before the covering was built. Frank Holt
Staunton, Virginia

The hotel at Seawright, partially completed in 1908, was to open in 1909 but was destroyed by fire eleven days before its scheduled opening.

David Schwartz
Staunton, Virginia

The covered spring and gazebo.

SEAWRIGHT SPRING

Old ornate concrete benches and tables stand as a reminder of unfulfilled plans.

The swimming pool, in use for many years, is now being filled in by the owners.

Stribling Springs

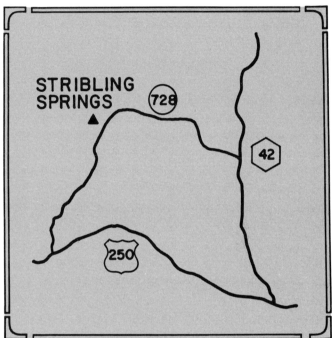

Located on C.R. 728, four miles north of U.S. 250, 13 miles northwest of Staunton, Augusta County.

Dr. Erasmus Stribling, the mayor and a prominent citizen of Staunton, opened Stribling Springs Inn in 1817. Stribling's Inn was very elegant for the area and offered the best of food and drink. Amusements were provided along with the usual health cures. There were three different springs—alum, sulphur and chalybeate, and 12 acres of lawn were included in the property's 1,400 acres.

People from all over the country and even from Europe flocked to this elegant resort in the mountains. Stribling's wife Matilda was a tremendous help in operating the spa and when she died, prior to the Civil War, Stribling lost interest and sold out to Chesley Kinney. Stribling died in 1858.

Beyer's rendering of Stribling Springs in his 1857 Album of Virginia.   VA

During the Civil War, the Inn was used as a military hospital. Gen. Stonewall Jackson used one of the houses near the Inn as his headquarters for a brief time. The Inn fell into disrepair after the war, and there is a court record of a forced sale in August 1878.

The resort must have been revived, however, as a 1915 brochure shows a hotel and a full-fledged resort. The brochure states that the resort was not a sanitarium, although a nearby physician is on call. No alcohol was sold within 15 miles.

Nothing remains of this once elegant resort that is sometimes referred to as Augusta Springs—a confusing element in the literature because there is another Augusta Springs to the south.

The hotel lawn at Stribling Springs from a 1915 brochure.   Waynesboro Public Library

The Stribling Springs Hotel around 1910. This is probably the original building built in 1817 by Erasmus Stribling.
David Schwartz
Staunton, Virginia

Sweet Chalybeate Springs

Located on S.R. 311 at the village of Sweet Chalybeate, Allegheny County, one mile east of Sweet Springs.

Although the springs were probably known and used by settlers in the 1700s, Sweet Chalybeate did not become a resort until 1836 when the Red Spring Company was incorporated. It had been called Red Sweet Springs for years and it was not until around 1900 that the name Sweet Chalybeate Springs came into popular use.

In about 1845 the property was acquired by John Sampson, who made improvements over the next several years. By 1850, under the ownership of Mr. C. Bias, the resort had become one of the most fashionable spas in Virginia. More than a million gallons of chalybeate water a day supplied the separate pools that Bias built for women and men. He also added a fine dining room and a reading

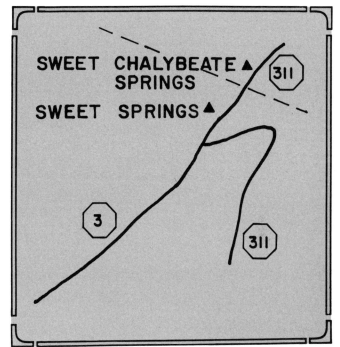

Beyer's rendering of Sweet Chalybeate (Red Sweet) Springs from his 1857 Album of Virginia. *VA*

room with newspapers—the only one of its kind in the mountains.

The springs were considered the strongest carbonated mineral water in the United States and a certain cure for sterility. Other spas in the area were bigger, and guests came for longer stays, but the Red Sweet was a favorite stopover for people, especially from South Carolina.

The resort did not make a comeback after the Civil War. The two closest spas, Sweet Springs and White Sulphur Springs, prospered, but Red Sweet slumbered along until it closed its doors in 1918.

Since then, the resort has had many owners. The buildings have been used as residences, and the main hotel housed a country store for many years.

In 1975, Sweet Chalybeate Inc. bought most of the old resort site and is attempting to restore it. The old pool and bath house have been refurbished and are open to the public. Just up from the pool sit a brick/frame cottage and a log cabin, probably old servants quarters. The original circular bandstand with a dome roof has been moved to a rise above the pool area. Both the north and south buildings that were sleeping rooms are still standing, separated by two square, frame cottages with pyramidal roofs. All of these buildings are still used as residences. The main hotel has recently been torn down to make way for a possible motel/restaurant.

The bandstand above the pool was moved from a site near the main hotel at the north end of the resort complex.

The South bay of sleeping rooms, two original cottages and the North bay of rooms at the extreme right are still standing and in use.   VA

The swimming pool and bath house at Sweet Chalybeate Springs have recently been refurbished. The bandstand, a brick/frame cottage and a log cabin sit on a rise above the pool.

Warm Springs

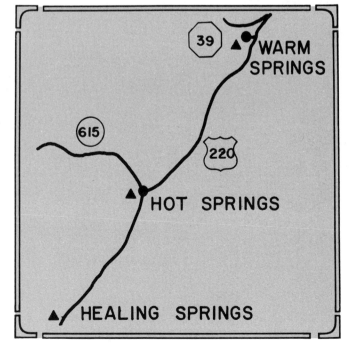

Located at the junction of S.R. 39 and U.S. 220 in Bath County five miles north of Hot Springs.

The Warm Springs have a temperature of 98 degrees and are the same type as the Hot Springs but contain a larger variety of mineral elements. According to legend the pools of hot water were discovered by an exhausted Indian runner in the sixteenth century.

Warm Springs history is tied in very closely with both Hot Springs and Healing Springs, as all three are in the Warm Springs Valley. People frequented the valley as early as the 1750s, and a 140-acre tract which included the springs was surveyed in 1751 for John Lewis and his son John. The younger Lewis settled the land and died there in 1788.

The men's pool/bath house, constructed in 1761, is one of the oldest spa structures still in existence. It is not quite as big as the women's pool/bath house, next to it, which was built in 1836.

In the old days, the common practice was to bathe in the pools twice a day, remaining in the water from 12 to 20 minutes each time and avoiding active exercise while in the water. It was thought that the best times for bathing were before breakfast and before dinner.

Apparently the first substantial structure built was the Colonnade, three stories high with a narrow terrace in front from which huge columns rose to a projection of the roof. It could have been erected around 1810-12. The larger "E" shaped hotel was built a few years later. It, too, was three stories high with only one bath tub in the building and two large outside toilets. Cottages were also built, which brought to more than 300 the number of people who could be housed at the resort. Many prominent persons were guests, including Thomas Jefferson, who spent considerable time here.

The years preceding the Civil War were the most popular for the spa, and John Brokenbrough was the owner from 1828 to 1852. After the war, Hot Springs became the most popular spa in the valley and Warm Springs declined rapidly.

The last individual owner was Colonel John L. Eubank, secretary of the Virginia Secession Convention of 1861. All three resorts in the Warm Springs Valley were consolidated under one ownership in 1890—the Virginia Hot Springs Company. For awhile Mrs. Eubank continued to operate Warm Springs under lease, but soon The Homestead at Hot Springs was the main attraction in the valley.

After Mrs. Eubank left, the company leased Warm Springs to others and then for some years tried to operate the resort with a manager, but it was a losing venture. At last, in 1924, the hotel was closed and it was razed in 1925.

Just south of the Warm Springs property, a private home was built in 1913 by Mary Johnston and later was remodeled as a resort hotel. It was called "Three Hills." In 1943 the Vichy French embassy staff was interned at the hotel but complained of its isolation and was eventually moved to the Cascades Inn at Healing Springs.

Today several cottages, one supposedly built before 1800, and the two bath houses are all that remain in the tranquil Warm Springs Valley. The town of Warm Springs is now the county seat of Bath County.

Beyer's rendering of Warm Springs from his 1857 Album of Virginia.   VA

Exterior of the men's pool/bath house built in 1761 and still in use. It is octagonal, 40 feet in diameter and 120 feet in circumference. It holds 43,000 gallons of water.

Exterior of the women's pool/bath house built in 1836 and still in use. It is 50 feet in diameter and 150 feet in circumference. It holds nearly 60,000 gallons of water.

The Warm Springs Hotel before 1925 when it was demolished. It had been built more than a hundred years before.
Bath County Historical Society

Interior of the men's pool/bath house. The temperature of the water is 98 degrees.

One of the original cottages thought to have been built in the 1760s is still in use. It is close to the old hotel site.

Washington Springs

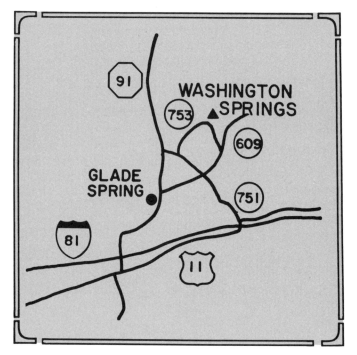

Located on C.R. 753 at the eastern edge of Washington County, two miles northeast of Glade Springs.

Washington Springs is at the southwestern edge of the Virginia spa region. Seven different springs were identified in the area— freestone, limestone, chalybeate, sulphur, arsenic, alum and magnesia.

The resort was built by Dr. Edmund Longley, who moved to the area from Maine because of his failing health. He discovered the springs, used the waters, and his health improved remarkably. He began to teach at Emory and Henry College and started construction of the resort sometime before the Civil War.

The original hotel contained about 20 rooms. A swimming pool was built behind the hotel, but it was later abandoned because of the improper cleaning facilities and the abun-

The dance pavillion still stands at the old resort site. Many a girl must have been whirled around the dance floor in the old days. Not much is left of this building today.

The Arsenic Springs at the Washington Springs resort in 1881.   VA

dance of copperhead snakes. There were also croquet lawns, tennis courts, a bowling alley built in the ravine beside the spring house and a dance pavilion which still remains.

After a 50-year association with the resort, Dr. Longley sold out to his son, and through the years the resort changed hands several times.

Around 1900 an addition was made to the hotel, and three guest cottages were built. From 1922 to 1936 James Broyles leased the property, but time was running out for the old, run-down buildings. A final try to recapture the earlier success of the resort was made in 1944, but it failed.

Then the first floor of the old hotel was used as apartments until 1975 when a fire, possibly set by an arsonist, burned down the building. The dance pavillion is still there—in a bad state of repair, and remains of the spring house and a reservoir can still be found in the ravine above the hotel site. The bowling alley was moved to McCall's Gap for use as a motel building.

The rest of the area is so overgrown it is hard to imagine that a resort with lush green lawns ever existed here.

The top of the Arsenic Springs spring house can still be seen in the dense undergrowth. It has been there for over 100 years.

George Thomas stands on the walkway to the hotel site, the only evidence of it left.

Wilson Springs

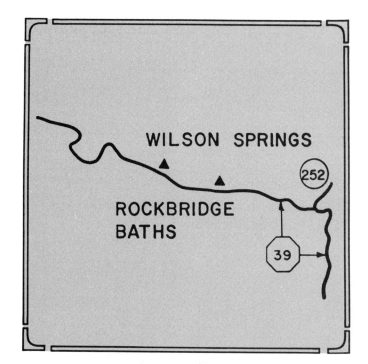

Located on S.R. 39 2 1/2 miles west of Rockbridge Baths and 13 miles northwest of Lexington, Rockbridge County.

Wilson Springs, or as it was once known, Strickler Springs, is unique—a sort of freak of nature—inasmuch as the spring rises on a tiny island in the middle of Maury River. A long, foot bridge built of logs made the island accessible.

William A. Wilson II bought 465 acres including the springs from Daniel Strickler in 1843 and moved to the farm the same year. In the following years the springs gradually came to be called Wilson Springs.

The first house had been built in 1775; Strickler added to it, and so did Wilson. People who came to the area because of the water would stay with the Wilsons at their house/hotel.

During the Civil War about 30 cabins were

Original cottages on the green of Wilson Springs. They were built during the Civil War at the east end of Goshen Pass.

built on the green opposite the sulphur spring at the east end of Goshen Pass. The cabins were used to quarter Confederate soldiers who guarded the Pass. These cabins later were called Wilson Row, and around them people of Rockbridge County built summer homes. The cabins, a few of which are still in use, were built on the Wilson land with only a gentleman's agreement and without any written contract.

Later the Wilsons built a bowling alley. At the height of the small resort's popularity, 250 people could stay in the cabins and 70 at the hotel. There was a freestone spring near the hotel, and the island spring was sulphurous.

In the middle of the green there was a pavillion where games were played and dances were held. Swimming, riding, fishing and picnicing kept the guests busy, and the resort was quite popular as a day picnic area.

Apparently the resort continued to operate into the 1920s. Today the two-story house/hotel is occupied by a Wilson descendant, and six of the cabins stand guard at the entrance to Goshen Pass. The rest were destroyed when S.R. 39 was relocated.

The Wilson Springs hotel along S.R. 39—now a private residence.

Yellow Sulphur Springs

Located four miles south of Blacksburg and four miles west of Christensburg, Montgomery County on C.R. 643.

Tucked away in an L-shaped valley is Yellow Sulphur Springs with a remarkable collection of existing resort buildings.

The site was probably discovered late in the eighteenth century. The land around it had been patented in 1751 by King George II to James Patton as part of a 7,500-acre domain. In 1800, Charles Taylor rented the site and constructed log buildings to accommodate the ill, who began to frequent the primitive resort. He purchased the spa and 160 acres in 1812. It was known as either "Yellow Springs" or "Taylor Springs" at this time.

Some building activity went on during the early 1800s, but the spa was eclipsed by the larger resorts to the north and east. It was a little more isolated, being at the western extreme of the main spa area. The large hotel which is still standing was built about 1810.

In 1842, Armistead W. Forrest bought the resort and 728 acres for $2,000. He improved and enlarged the main hotel and began construction of cottage row.

With the coming of a railroad to the area in the 1850s, business at the spa increased sharply. In 1853, a syndicate bought the resort and added "Sulphur" to the name. They built a turnpike from the Christianburg Depot, and in 1855 the Yellow Sulphur Springs Company was formed. Buildings were further improved and the spa became increasingly important.

Several groups owned the spa just before and after the Civil War. The spa reopened around 1868 and Edward A. Pollard wrote of it in his book *The Virginia Tourist* in 1870: "The accommodations of this spring are as yet limited, their capacity scarcely exceeding a hundred persons. But the buildings are new and comfortable, and the table furnished by the proprietors is one of the best in the moun-

tains. . .The grounds have a natural beauty to which architectural designs (however we might wish an extension of buildings for the accommodations of a larger number of visitors) are not necessary to add."

A new 40-room hotel was built in 1871 by the new owners, J.J. Wade and J. Wade, but it burned to the ground in 1873, and the resort slipped into a decade of financial difficulty.

Captain Ridgway Holt purchased the property in 1886 and immediately invested a large amount in new buildings. He built a 60-room hotel just down the access road from the main buildings.

Many of the old Confederate leaders visited the springs after the war. Jubal Early, who suffered from chronic dyspepsia, had visited the spa before the war and returned to make it his summer home. In those days old Confederates would take over the town of Christiansburg for a celebration, and the towns-

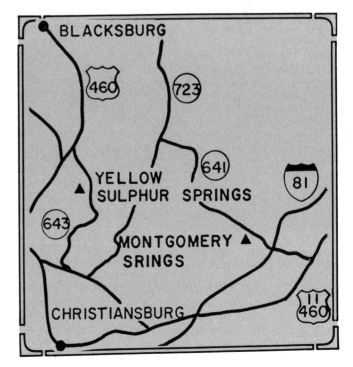

people seemed to enjoy it as much as the old soldiers.

For awhile, the resort enjoyed considerable success, but by 1917 business had almost ceased, and it closed for good in 1923.

In 1932 the Yellow Sulphur Springs Recreation Sanitorium, Inc. was organized to turn the resort into a sort of nursing home. The Depression, however, prevented this venture from materializing. Later in the year the resort was taken over by the Virginia Transient Bureau, and a home for homeless men was established. The buildings and grounds were restored in the next three years.

Mrs. Charles C. Lester, the daughter of Charles A. Crumpacker, the last owner, now makes her home at the old spa and lives among some wonderful memories and artifacts of a grand part of the history of this area.

Beyer's rendering of Yellow Sulphur Springs from his 1857 Album of Virginia.   VA

The second hotel built at the Springs in 1871. It burned to the ground in 1873. It had 40 rooms plus a ballroom, dining room, bar room and billiard room.   VA

The original hotel, which dates in part from 1810. Restored through the years, it is now in bad repair.

The ornate spring house, which has been altered but is still standing, and the original hotel in the background are pictured in this stereoptican view in 1872.   VA

The third hotel at the Springs. Built in 1886, it stood until the 1940s, many years after the resort ceased to operate.   Virginia Tech Archives

Remains of the third hotel's foundation, on the road leading to the main resort complex.

The spring house. Although altered considerably since the 1870s, it is still in good condition.

A row of long, low cottages built in the typical style of the day. Built in 1842 on a hill overlooking the resort. They appear to be in good condition.

The bowling alley up the ravine from the main building sags considerably, but appears to be set up for yet another bowling frame.

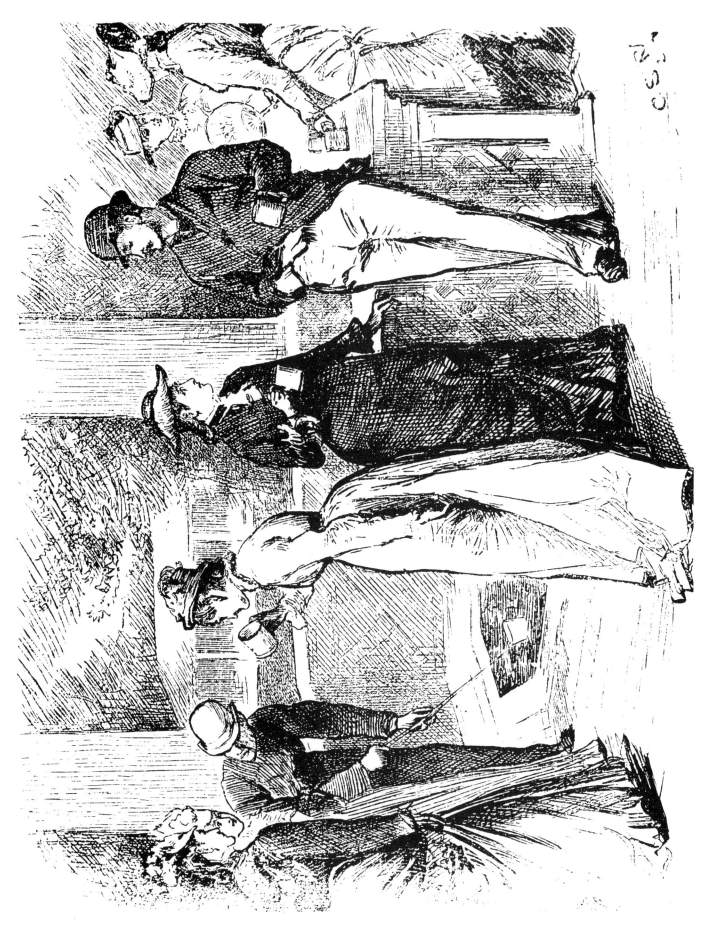

DRINKING THE WATER AT THE SPRING.

West Virginia Springs

The Importance

*of using a pure
water to prevent*

Typhoid Fever and other diseases

As the healthy adult requires about from 70 to 100 oz. of water daily for the processes of nutrition, about ⅓ of which is contained in articles of diet and ⅔ in the form of liquids, it is a matter of the deepest consideration that the water used for drinking purposes should be of the purest form, owing to the many severe diseases propagated by pollution of same. The three main sources of pollution are found—first, excess in mineral matter, second, vegetable, and third, animal or organic. The last of the three being the most dangerous of said group as it plays an important part in causing such diseases as **CHOLERA, TYPHOID FEVER, DIPHTHERIA, DYSENTERY, DIARRHEA, &c.** With regard to public supplies it may be stated generally, that water may become polluted either at its source, in the course of distribution, or through defects connected with its storage, as supplies taken from rivers is suspicious even after filtering, owing to the sourage of towns up streams. Deep wells may become polluted by the entrance of surface impurities. But the most frequent source of pollution to which public supplies are exposed are those dependent in the arrangement for distribution and storage, as for example, in a good many houses the same cistern is used to supply the closets as well as for drinking purposes and the sewer gas has access to the surface water in the cistern. The above and innumerable other ways often take part in rendering water unfit for use.

Concerning the **Virginia Magnesian Alkaline Water** the consumer of same can avoid the many above risks set forth as I can fully recommend it as to its purity, medicinal properties and softness, making it a beneficial as well as an agreeable table water by aiding digestion and facilitating the action of the kidneys and liver.

J. B. CATLETT, M. D.

(Reference Wilson Hygiene.)

Can furnish water by the month so low that every family
can afford to use it for table purposes.

Thos. Hogshead,
MANAGER.

Staunton, Va.

Barger (Greenbrier) Springs

Located on S.R. 17, three miles south of Talcott, Summers County.

This small resort in southeastern West Virginia had the distinction of being the site of the first store in this part of the state. Around 1800, Isaac Carden settled in the area and established a business catering to the local trappers and hunters. His goods came up the James River and Kanawha Canal from Richmond to Buchanan, Virginia and then went by wagon over the mountains to Carden's Springs, as it was known then.

Years later, William Barger, who had married Carden's daughter, inherited the springs area but did nothing to build it up as a resort. He used it only as a farm. The log cabins that had been built in the early 1800s for local people to stay in while taking the waters were falling into disrepair.

The Barger family farmed the area until 1903 when a group of 30 men from Hinton formed a company to buy the springs and build summer homes for themselves. The property consisted of 315 acres on the Greenbrier River, back of Big Bend Tunnel Mountain.

They put a new covering, which is still in place, over the original springs, and built eight cottages. The property was surveyed and 30 lots laid out. In 1905 a hotel was built and the springs became a popular site for the local people.

By 1929, the hotel closed, and the area again receded into oblivion. Today, many of the cottages—lined up along S.R. 17—are still in use, and water still issues forth under the spring house just off the highway.

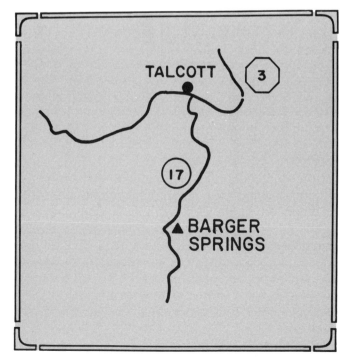

Spring house at Barger Springs. This covering of a tin roof supported by concrete columns was built about 1903 to replace an earlier one.

Original cottages built as early as 1903 still remain and are in use along S.R. 17 at Barger Springs.

Berkeley (Bath) Springs

Located in the town of Berkeley Springs, Morgan County.

The town of Berkeley Springs, or Bath, as it was known for years, can trace its history back perhaps thousands of years to when the Indians used the warm waters for medicinal purposes. These waters seemed to help their rheumatism which was a very common ailment. Indian tribes from the Great Lakes to the Carolinas, including the Six Nations, the Delawares, the Tuscaroras and the Catawbas, came to the springs, and although they were eternally at war with one another, they established a truce in regard to the area around the springs so that all might benefit.

Recorded history of the locale goes back to 1730 when the European settlers came to use the water as the Indians did. In 1748, at age 16, George Washington was sent here as part of a survey party because this was the western limit of Lord Fairfax's land grant (originally given in 1681 by Charles II of England to Lord Hapton).

Washington returned here often through

the years, and in 1761 he wrote: "I think myself benefitted by the water and am not without hope of their making a cure for me." He had a cottage built at the springs which he used during his presidency, and this could be considered the first summer White House.

The springs issue from the base of a steep ridge rising about 450 feet above the valley. They discharge from five principal sources and numerous lesser ones all within 100 yards of each other. They flow at 2,000 gallons per minute at a uniform temperature of 74.3°F.

Originally the site had been called Warm Springs. In October 1776, the General Assembly of Virginia passed an act establishing the town as Bath in what was then Berkeley County. (Berkeley County was formed from Frederick County in 1722.) The town was named for the famous spa in England in the hope that some of the glitter would rub off and patrons would flock there. A board of trustees was formed and lots were laid out for sale. some people also referred to the town as Berkeley Springs.

However, Bath County subsequently was formed, and the county seat was called Warm Springs. All of this name duplication caused such confusion, and postal errors became so frequent, that the name Berkeley Springs was adopted about 1863. The present county of Morgan was established in 1820.

Many famous people of the day frequented the small town and resort, and in the late 1780s a building boom began. James Rumsey, a then famous inventor and one of the first to build a successful steamboat, was in charge of some of the construction.

The restort continued to be a well-known and popular spot for both invalids and pleasure seekers. Gambling, dancing and horse racing were favorite amusements. People came from Virginia, Maryland and Washington although it was hard to get there because of poor roads. In 1843, the Baltimore and Ohio Railroad reached Hancock, Maryland, and it became much easier for people from the east to reach the resort.

Between 1845 and 1848, Colonel John Strother constructed a large hotel with room for 400 guests. He called it "The Pavillion Hotel" and later "The Strother Hotel" and finally "The Berkeley Springs Hotel."

During the Civil War, the resort, like most others was closed and suffered from the ravages of both armies. But in 1869, the large hotel was purchased by a Baltimore company,

refitted and refurnished, and the resort again took on an air of prosperity. In 1876 John Trego, of Baltimore, purchased the resort. The railroad reached the springs with a branch line in 1888, and it could bring guests directly to the resort. Some of the wealthy came in their own private rail cars.

Then in 1898 the lavish hotel burned to the ground, and in 1901 another large hotel, the Fairfax Inn, also was destroyed. With these calamities the resort and town began a rapid decline. Competition from bigger and more fancy resorts also played a role.

The West Virginia Department of Public Institutions owned the park for years until it was transferred to the Department of Natural Resources in 1970. It was the first state park in the nation and is now part of the West Virginia state parks system. Of the scores of resorts built, it is the one still in existence that emphasizes health treatments.

The Country Inn on the old hotel site was built in 1933 by Mr. and Mrs. Walter Harmison. Wings were added in 1937. The new bath house, also at the old hotel site, was built in 1929. At one time there were separate, covered swimming pools for men and women, but the pools were converted into one larger one, and in 1950 the covers were razed. The Roman bath house, built in 1784 by James Rumsey, is still standing. It was once the ladies' shower bath, and is now a tool shed.

Although not a part of the resort proper, "The Castle," a half-scale replica of Berkeley Castle in England is worth mentioning. It was built in 1886-1889 by Col. Samuel Taylor Suit

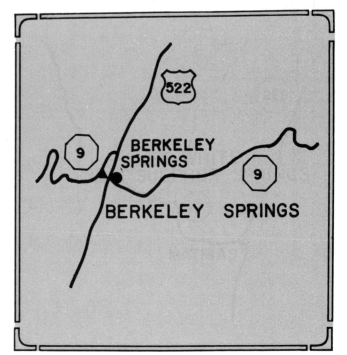

for his young bride, Rosa Pelham. He died before the castle overlooking the town was completed, but Mrs. Suit lived there for years, giving lavish parties until her inheritance money ran out. The building is now open as a tourist attraction.

Berkeley Springs is one of the oldest, if not the oldest, health spa in the Virginias. The following is a reference to it which appeared in a Richmond newspaper on June 19, 1784:

"The histories of the most eminent empires cannot produce more flattering or greater instances of the genius of a people proud to cultivate the arts and eloquences of polite refinement in the infancy of its national existence, that is, in a state of freedom, than in the United States of America. Among the various exertions that legislative wisdom and well-directed policy pervading the whole for the permanent establishment of general good and national grandeur, we are happy to find that the convenience of a medicinal bath, supported on a plan of propriety and decorum, has engaged the attention of the public. Popular respect will determine whether this place can have for its basis the uses of similar springs in Europe.

"In Berkely County five bathing-houses, with adjacent dressing-rooms, are already completed; an assembly-room and theater are also constructed for the innocent and rational amusements of the polite who may assemble there.

"The American company of comedians it is expected will open here, under the direction of Mr. Ryan, on the 15th of July, and to continue till the 1st of September. It is supposed they will prove so acceptable to the bath as to encourage the proprietor to renew his visits yearly.

"'The muses follow freedom,' said Socrates. From Greece to Rome they certainly fled when those mighty empires fell. Let us hail, therefore, their residence in America."

A rendering of the Pavillion from Moorman's book. VA

Strother's hotel, the Pavillion, was built in the 1840s and burned down in 1898.

Frederick Newbraugh
Berkeley Springs, W. Va.

Views of the resort in 1906. The pagoda over the spring in the bottom picture was torn down many years ago. The buildings to the right are the swimming pool and the bath house.

WASHINGTON STREET. BERKELEY SPRINGS, W. VA.

The Country Inn, built in 1933 with additions in 1936. The original Strother Hotel occupied part of this site.

Frederick Newbraugh
Berkeley Springs, W. Va.

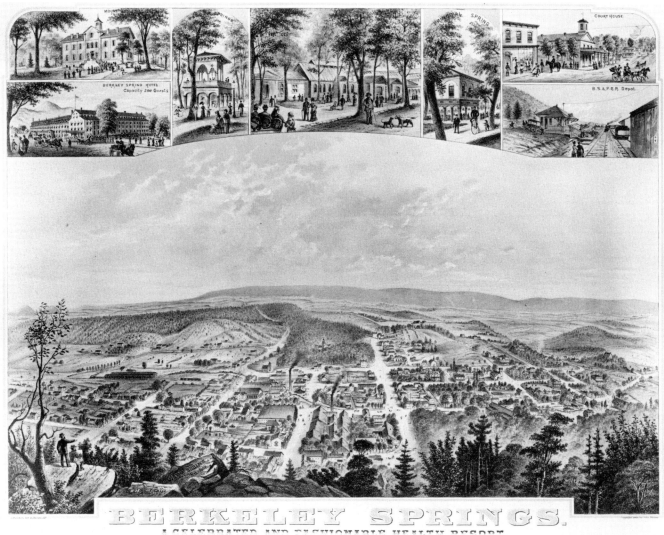

PAVILION HOTEL.

The Proprietors' Treat

BILL OF FARE.

For Saturday 29th Aug 1846

Venison & wild Turkey
Rabbit a la Daub
squirrels in Chalon

ROAST MUTTON.
Roast Beef & Cakes
BOILED MUTTON. *& Cakes*

ROASTED *Pheasants*

BOILED CHICKENS.

Green Turtle
in Steak
Welsh Rare bits

TOMATOES.

GREEN CORN.

RICE.

POTATOES.

BEETS.

Cauliflower
Lima Beans

DESERT.

Frozen Custard
Ice cream
Peaches & cream

THE BAR.

—:o:—

OLD MADERIA.

PALE SHERRY.

BROWN SHERRY.

OLD PORT.

CHAMPAIGN, *Star Brand.*

CLARETT.

PORTER.

SCOTCH ALE.

BROWN STOUT.

OLD RYE.

P & D BRANDY.

OLD PEACH.

IRISH WHISKEY.

Bill of fare of the Pavillion in 1846.

Frederick Newbraugh
Berkeley Springs, W. Va.

Gen. David Hunter Strother's home in Berkeley Springs. Strother was a well-known writer and illustrator for Harper's Monthly (under the pseudonym "Porte Crayon"), a Union officer during the Civil War and an important citizen of Berkeley Springs. His father had built the Pavillion in the 1840s. Frederick Newbraugh
Berkeley Springs, W. Va.

Berkeley Springs State Park showing the spring house and old bath house with the spring pool in the foreground.
State of West Virginia

Old Roman bath house and gentlemen's spring in the Berkeley Springs State Park.

State of West Virginia
Historic Preservation Unit

A bandstand at Berkeley Springs State Park.

State of West Virginia

The last remaining building built by James Rumsey in the 1780s. (He invented the steamboat in 1787.) The building was originally the ladies' shower bath but has been altered considerably through the years. It is now a tool shed.

View of the bath house built in 1929 and the enclosed spring water. Legend has it that the small pool next to the stone wall was used by George Washington, but this is highly questionable.

FAIRFAX SPRING.

THE ARRIVAL.

INTERIOR GENT'S BATH.

PAGODA, OR GENT'S SPRING.

INTERIOR GENT'S POOL.

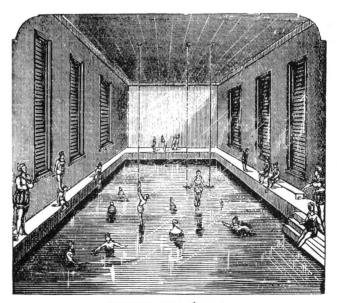

INTERIOR LADIES' POOL.

Blue Sulphur Springs

Located on C.R. 25, 4 miles south of Smoot, Greenbrier County.

Blue Sulphur Springs, along with the White, the Red, the Salt and the Sweet, was one of the favorite and most fashionable spas of the pre-Civil War days. It was located on Kitchen Creek in a valley on the western side of Muddy Creek Mountain. The main road that went by it had been an early buffalo and Indian trail which later became the main highway from the southeast to Kanawha Falls and the Ohio River.

James Patterson obtained a patent to 490 acres including the spring site from the State of Virginia in 1789. The spring came out of the ground in a flat field instead of at or near the base of a .mountain. It was a strong sulphur water and was supposed to be a good remedy for liver and skin diseases, irritations of the kidneys, bladder and prostate gland and irregular menstration.

Patterson's daughter became owner of the 24 1/2 acres including the spring, which came to be known locally as Nancy Patterson Sulphur Springs. Anson Allen was granted a license for the first hotel there around 1829.

A charter company, the Blue Sulphur Springs Company, was formed in 1834 to build a resort. George Washington Buster became the sole owner and commenced to build a large hotel and other typical spa facilities. The resort was named Blue Sulphur, reportedly, because the spring pool seemed to be as "blue as the Sea of Galilee."

The main hotel was built of brick, three stories high, 180 feet long by 50 feet wide. A 12 foot piazza ran across the full length. A two story wing was added to each side. The main building contained a large dining room and two receiving rooms, a ballroom, bar and chambers. Over 200 guests could be accommodated. Many brick and frame cottages were added along with servants' quarters and stables. A marble spring house was built

facing the hotel. It was truly a magnificent spa for its day.

In 1840, Dr. Alexis Martin, who had been a surgeon in Napoleon's Army came to the spa to be its resident physician. Bath houses were built and the first mud baths in the United States were introduced here. Dr. Martin built up a fast reputation for the healing powers of the Blue's waters.

The spa was staffed mainly with Buster's own slaves. Its visitors included people from all over the world, among them such American and foreign dignitaries as Andrew Jackson, Henry Clay, Robert E. Lee and Jerome Bonaparte, Napoleon's brother. The Blue was on the spa circuit for the rich and famous of the day.

Not everybody, however, was impressed with it. William Burke, who traveled the spring circuit in the 1840s and wrote his *Mineral Springs of Virginia* in 1846 had the following description of the spa:

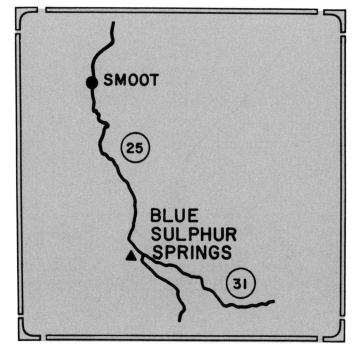

"We said that this valley is beautiful; we should, perhaps, have said, it has been. *Fuit Illuim.* Never have we seen bad taste more unfortunately illustrated than here. It seems as if the designer had his brain *obfuscated* by mint-julep. What man in his sober senses could have ever thought of spoiling a lovely valley like this, admitting a prospect of several miles, by throwing across it from hill to hill a long line of buildings which could have been so easily and so gracefully ranged along the sides; not only obstructing the view, but also preventing the delightful current of air which otherwise would have fanned it in the dog-days. Not content with this piece of botching, they must permit Dr. Martin to erect his *tartanean orens* also across the valley, leaving the Temple containing the Spring, and the lawn in which it stands, bounded by brick walls and mountains."

Business started to decline in the late 1850s due to competition, economics of the country and the mounting internal strife. The Baptist Church in western Virginia at this time wanted to establish a private school and a school to educate ministers. In 1858 the Western Virginia Baptist Association met to establish Allegheny High School. Several towns offered sites, but in 1859 the Association bought Blue Sulphur Springs for $44,000. The school opened on Oct. 1, 1859, and later was called Allegheny College.

Misfortune, however, struck the school in September 1860 when a fire burned the main hotel to the ground. Part of the hotel was rebuilt in late 1860 and a large number of students were expected to enroll in 1861. But with gathering war clouds in the South, the students started leaving to join the Confederate Army and later in 1861 the college ceased to exist.

During the war, the spa was home to both armies and used as a hospital. In the winter of 1862-63, several hundred Georgia troops were encamped there. Eighty-nine of them died of a typhoid fever epidemic and were buried on top of the hill in coffins made out of benches from the cottages and buildings of the resort. The United Daughters of the Confederacy placed a fence around the graves, but all trace of the site has disappeared. In 1864, Union troops burned down the rest of the buildings, and the spa lay in ashes never to rise again.

This, however, was not to be the end of the story. In 1878 heirs of G.W. Buster regained title to the property inasmuch as the defunct

Drawing of Blue Sulphur Springs from Moorman's book The Virginia Springs, *1859. VA*

college did not make its mortgage payment. In 1906, three trustees of the new Baptist, Alderson Academy sued the U.S. Government for damages incurred during the war on Allegheny College. They won their case but were never paid the money.

In the Congress of the United States in 1937, Representative John Kee presented a bill (H.R. 2084) to make payment to the Baptist Association, 73 years after the spa was burned by Union troops. Again money was never paid, possibly because the statute of limitations had run out.

All that is left now of the famous spa located in its isolated, pristine valley is a stately Grecian Temple over the spring which still runs in a pasture. The present owners rebuilt the roof in 1966.

Beyer's rendering of Blue Sulphur Springs from his Album of Virginia. *1857.* VA

The Grecian Temple over the spring is all that remains of this once famous spa.

Capon Springs

Located on C.R. 16/3 four miles east of S.R. 259 in the extreme southeast corner of Hampshire County.

It is located on a deep narrow glen on the west side of the Great North Mountain. The springs rise at the base of a huge vertical outcrop of sandstone.

The site was first discovered by Henry Frye, pioneer settler of the Capon area, in 1765. While hunting one day on the mountain side, near the springs, he killed a large bear. Starting back to camp with a portion of the bear, he became thirsty. He began to look for water, found the springs, and suspected their medicinal value because of the peculiar taste and temperature of the water. The next summer his wife became ill and Frye decided to take her to the springs for a possible cure. He built a small cabin, the first building at the site. His wife was subsequently cured of her rheumatism, and the place for many years was known as Frye's Springs.

In October 1787, 20 acres of land around and including the spring was laid out into lots and streets. The fledgling town set up a Board of Trustees, made improvements, and began to become a resort as the springs became popular with visitors, many from the surrounding area. A small boarding house was built along with 18 cottages.

By 1849 the place had become so popular that a company was formed to construct a large hotel. The idea was to make Capon Springs one of the grand resorts of the Virginias. The completed hotel, known as the "Mountain House" was one of the largest structures in the South. It was four stories high, 262 feet by 190 feet, with a large portico, 175 feet long by 18 feet wide. The front of the portico was set off with huge Doric pillars, 35 feet high. Five hundred people could be accommodated in the building with a seating capacity in the dining room of 600.

Facing the hotel was the bath house, 280 feet long, containing 40 bath rooms, hot and cold plunges and shower baths. The swimming pool, at 90 feet by 48 feet, was the largest in Virginia.

At the head of the glen in which the buildings were situated, the main spring poured out from the base of the mountain at 6,000 gallons per hour. Its temperature was 64°, and it was known to contain alkaline lithia, soda, magnesia, bromine, iodine and carbonic acid. These substances are alkaloid carbonates which make the springs similar in medical effect to those at Vichy, France and Carlsbad, Germany.

Many famous people visited the resort before the Civil War. They could take the train to Capon Station, sixteen miles away and then take a stagecoach to the springs. Robert E. Lee and his wife were visting the spa in 1859 when he was called to go to Harpers Ferry to put down the attack by John Brown.

In 1861 with the war coming and the resort

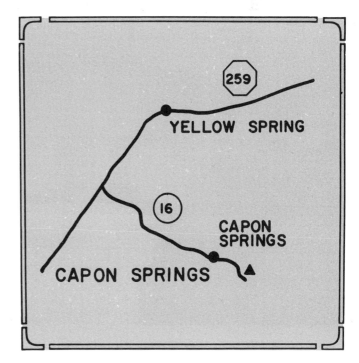

$8,000 in debt, the state ordered the place sold. However, the new state of West Virginia took it over during the war, and Capon Springs became part of the debt that West Virginia owed Virginia after the war.

The spa continued to operate after the war, but the Mountain House burned down in 1911. Sometime later some of the existing buildings were built. At present the well known spa is one of three still operating in the state. It is a private health and recreation resort; guests may stay there only on the recommendation of other guests. The buildings and grounds are in excellent condition and there seems to be an ample amount of business.

A letter in the *Baltimore Sun*, July 14, 1851 described Capon Springs:

"Above the spring, peaks tower in the most eccentric shapes...Sometimes one shoots up perpendicularly, while another leans like an Italian tower. The grouping of the whole bears the most extraordinary resemblence to a ruined castle, such as the Rhine affords...When the sun is shining brightly over a blue sky, and its rays fall with full effect upon the peaks, their hues change from their general gray to pure white, and so varied and tossing are their shapes that they seem to be snowy masses of vapor, rising over the trees and relieved against the azure heaven...and again, when the sunset throws its hues over the entire scene, these rocks become tinged with the hues of parting day...while among the masses of rock that lie scattered around the pavillion, the richest variety of trees and shrubs spring almost with the luxuriance of the tropics and mingle their own brightest verdue with the fleeting colors of the sky."

BATH HOUSES.　　　CAPON SPRINGS.　　　CAPON SPRINGS HOTEL.

View of the "Mountain House" to the right and the bath houses to the left in the 1860s.
Virginia Tech Archives

Swimming pool at Capon Springs.

-146-

MUSIC STAND & SPRING.

CAPON.

CAPON LAKE.

Views of Capon Springs from a Baltimore and Ohio pamphlet in 1883. VA

Main building and office at Capon Springs.

One of the guest lodges at Capon Springs.

Lee White Sulphur Springs

Located five miles west of Mathias, Hardy County on C.R. 12 at Lost River State Park.

The springs is another resort that was originally part of the large Fairfax Grant. At the close of the Revolutionary War, Lord Fairfax's Grant was confiscated. The state of Virginia divided it and deeded it to soldiers of the American Army. In 1796, more than 44,000 acres including the springs area was given to Light Horse Harry (Henry) Lee, father of Confederate General Robert E. Lee.

Light Horse Harry built a boarding house at the site. In about 1800 he also built a cabin, which is still standing and is called the Lee Cabin, where he spent considerable time. Sometime after 1800, he reportedly built a large, two-story log hotel, 100 feet by 49 feet, with a fireplace at each end.

When the elder Lee died in 1818, the sons and daughters inherited the springs. They conveyed them in 1832 to Charles Carter Lee, and he later transferred 493 acres to his son, George T. Lee, the last of the Lee family to own the spa. George maintained a private resort there for his friends for many years.

The springs had been named for John Howard in the early 1700s, but when Carter Lee leased the area to Cyrus Hulton in 1851, he called it Hardy White Sulphur Springs.

From 1860 to 1862 the property was unoccupied. McNeill's Rangers, a Confederate partisan group, used the area frequently on its forays in the Valley of Virginia and the South Branch Valley. Then about 1862 Mr. Perry Cooper undertook the operation of the hotel and stayed on until 1887. In the meantime, as the war continued, residents of Moorefield and vicinity moved here to escape the war and established a sort of refugee camp.

In 1879, M.S. Alexander bought the springs at an auction and improved the buildings and grounds. He in turn sold out to H.S. Carr in 1887 for $1,000. Carr developed the area into a large summer resort in the 1890s, enlarging and remodeling the hotel and adding bowling alleys, tennis courts, hot and cold sulphur baths and telephones. He renamed the spa Lee White Sulphur Springs.

A brochure put out by Carr in 1897 expounded on the virtues of the waters there. It read in part:

"Of the purest white sulphur, they rise from a bed of solid rock, and are of a temperature unequalled by any other sulphur springs, being uniformly fifty-two degrees Fahrenheit at all seasons of the year—ten degrees colder than the celebrated 'Greenbrier White Sulphur Springs.' By analysis they are shown to be medicinally superior to the 'Greenbrier White,' containing no lime and a larger percent of soda than any other sulphur springs known in the Virginias. They eliminate thoroughly all impurities from the system; act powerfully on the urinary organs, and speedily relieve dyspepsia, owing chiefly perhaps, to the large amount of soda contained in them.

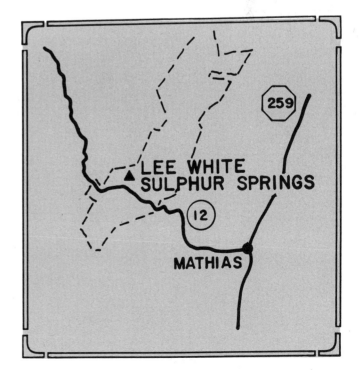

Remarkable cures of kidney disease, dyspepsia and diseases of malarial origin have been effected by these waters, and they have proved especially beneficial in invigorating the system after depletion from excessive use of alcoholic stimulants."

The spa continued to prosper until 1910 when the hotel burned down. In 1934 the State of West Virginia took over the property and developed it into a state park with the help of the Civilian Conservation Corps.

Today the park includes 3,712 acres of beautiful woods and lawns and is called Lost River State Park. The Lee cabin is now a museum and is listed on the National Register of Historic Places.

A rustic spring house is located across from the Lee cabin.

The Lee cabin at Lost River State Park was built around 1800 by Light Horse Harry Lee, owner of the springs.

Minnehaha Springs

Located on S.R. 39 at Minnehaha Springs, Pocahontas County, nine miles east of Marlinton.

No longer a health spa, the resort is used now as a summer camp for boys.

Minnehaha Springs is located where the waters of Douthard's Creek empty into Knapp's Creek, near the base of the Allegheny Mountain. The elevation is 2,300 feet.

Settlers had farmed the rich bottomlands for many years, but development of the resort was a fairly recent occurrence. The water, found on the farm of the Lockridge family, was analogous to the water of Hot Springs. The name Minnehaha Springs was given to it because of Indian relics found near it. There is also conjecture that Pocahontas, the Indian princess, might have lived in the area.

A company known as the Pocahontas Mineral Water Development Company was organized; a hotel was completed on top of the hill above the spring in 1914, and a bath house with an inside pool was built at the bottom. Management was turned over to the owners of the Casa Ybel, a winter resort in Florida.

The two-story hotel had 24 bedrooms. A 1914 brochure states that it had its own electric and water plant, modern plumbing, running water and call bells in each room and was comfortably furnished throughout. There were automobiles to drive guests to and from

The hotel in 1916 overlooked the springs from its hilltop location. It was constructed in 1914 and burned down in 1945. The dining hall for Camp Minnehaha now sits on the site.

James Worth
Minnehaha Springs, W. Va.

Marlinton, the nearest railroad station.

Fishing, horseback riding, tennis, dancing, pool and cards were optional amusements along with bathing in the mineral water. The brochure stated, however, that it should be clearly understood that the resort was not intended for the treatment or cure of serious ailments, but was strictly a summer resort. It was also advised that patients consult their own physician before using the springs for medicinal or therapeutic reasons.

It is not certain when the resort was closed to the public but in 1944 a summer camp for boys was established, called Camp Minnehaha. On Feb. 4, 1945 the hotel burned to the ground destroying all its contents. The bath house was moved to a place opposite the pool. It is now used as a gym and recreational hall for the camp. The pool is still in use. A dining hall and other structures were built for camp use.

The bath house and inside pool at Minnehaha Springs in 1916, two years after it was built.

James Worth
Minnehaha Springs, W. Va.

The bath house, moved off the pool and placed opposite it, is now used as a gym for Camp Minnehaha.

The pool, constructed in 1914, is still in use by Camp Minnehaha.

The spring enclosure at Minnehaha Springs.

Pence Springs

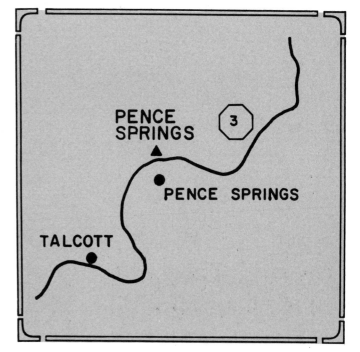

Located on S.R. 3 at the village of Pence Springs, Summers County, 12 miles east of Hinton.

Buffalo frequented the springs long before white settlers came. The original patent on the property was held by William Kincaide and later by Jesse Beard. The first hotel was built in 1872 and was sold in 1878 by Beard's heirs to Andrew Pence, who later made additions to it.

Then about 1900 another large hotel, "The Valley Heights," was built nearby by E.M. Carney. He bored a number of wells abound Pence's property in order to pump the sulphur water. This resulted in a law suit in 1904—Pence *vs.* Carney—to enjoin the pumping and the wasting of water by Carney. The court, however, decided that Carney had the right to pump the water in a reasonable way which would not be harmful to Pence's operation.

In 1918, another hotel was built along S.R. 3. This building was purchased in 1947 by the State of West Virginia for use as a woman's prison. And now it is being restored to serve its original function—as a hotel.

The old hotel at Pence Springs. It was built in 1918.

The spring house at Pence Springs on the property of a campground which has a large weekly flea market. The house was built in the 1870s.

Red Sulphur Springs

Located on S.R. 12 at Red Sulphur Springs, Monroe County, 18 miles south of Hinton.

On the social circuit before the Civil War, Red Sulphur Springs had been known as a watering place since about 1800. The first people visited the area to cure their itch, sore legs and diseases of the skin by drinking the sulphur water and rubbing it on their skins.

The waters from the springs empty into Fritz Run about 250 feet from the spring. Fritz Run flows into Indian Creek approximately one-fourth mile west. A pavillion over the springs was erected about 1830, and the resort began to attract people.

Dr. William Burke of Alabama and Richmond bought the valley and sulphur springs in 1833. He envisioned a large resort, which he built and later described in these words: "In extent of accommodations, it is sufficient for 350 persons. The improvements consist of the hotel, 80 by 42 feet, two stories containing dining room, drawing rooms, bar and storage rooms, etc., with a double piazza the whole length; Alabama Row 300 feet long, with a piazza the whole length, and a neat two story building at one end; Philadelphia Row, 200 feet long, with a piazza; Bachelor's Row, 104 feet long; Carolina House, 112 feet long and two stories high. Between the last ranges is a house for the reception of visitors on their arrival. There is a continuous piazza from the extreme end of Philadelphia Row to that of Carolina House, 471 feet in length.

"Above Bachelor's Row, on a terrace, is Society Hall, 80 by 42 feet, two stories and basement, having a portico supported by nine Ionic columns 25 feet presenting a very imposing front from the valley. Besides these ranges, there are numerous cottages and offices and at the entrance a mercantile establishment; but the structure most deserving of notice is the Pavillion over the spring."

Although the resort was somewhat isolated in Monroe County, people continued to come from all parts of the country by railroad, boat and stagecoach. Railroads were getting closer to the West Virginia spas in the 1850s, but they did not get into Monroe County until 1873. After that it was much easier to reach the resort.

Dr. Burke sold his beloved spa before the Civil War to the Campbell Brothers.

Famous people who visited the spa included a future Chief Justice of the Supreme Court, Roger Taney, who brought his ailing wife, and Francis Scott Key was also a visitor.

Like most of the other resorts in western Virginia, Red Sulphur lost patrons during the Civil War, and it saw service as a hospital. After the war, the resort changed hands several times, and in 1890 the property was conveyed to the Red Sulphur Springs Company. Shortly thereafter, Levi Morton, a banker, congressman and vice president under President Benjamin Harrison, pur-

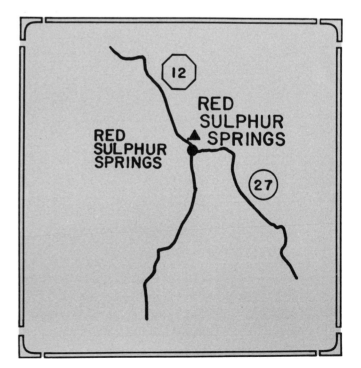

chased the resort. He built a new dining room, bath houses and bowling alley, and he had a telephone line installed to connect the spa to nearby Talcott. The old hotel held 400 guests and board was then $10 to $17 a week.

But business was not what it had been in the old days, and Morton tried to give the resort to the state for use as a tuberculosis sanitarium. When the state turned him down, he sold it in 1915 to a group of investors. They tried to operate it again but were unable to make a go of it and during World War I sold out to Judge C.W. Campbell. He tore down all the buildings and divided the property into numerous tracts. Thus another of the antebellum circuit spas passed into oblivion.

All that is left of Red Sulphur—a stone spring enclosure.

Beyer's rendering of Red Sulphur Springs from his 1857 Album of Virginia.   VA

Salt Sulphur Springs

Located on U.S. 219 three miles south of Union, Monroe County.

Salt Sulphur Springs is one of the most visible of the major springs/health spas. As one approaches the site from the north, a large stone building, originally the hotel, stands at the bend in the road to mark the site of this once grand resort.

Salt Sulphur lies in a rather shallow ravine with Indian Creek cutting through it. The resort capitalized on three springs—the Iodine, Salt Sulphur and Sweet. The waters were advertised as a remedy for "chronic diseases of the brain" such as "headaches, incipient mania and local palsy dependent upon congestion or chronic inflammation." They were also used as cures for neuralgia and other ailments of the day.

When William Shanks received a grant of 595 acres of land on Indian Creek in 1787, it probably never occurred to him that his quiet farm would someday become a noted Southern resort. One of the springs—Sweet Sulphur—was discovered about 1803 and Salt Sulphur in 1805. For years afterward, only a few dwellings were built and few people used the mineral waters. The stone bath house still standing at the entrance to the resort, was built about 1820.

Ervin Benson bought the potential resort site in 1797, and two early guests to the springs, Issac Caruthers and William Erskine, ended up marrying Benson's daughters. These two brothers-in-law took over the fledgling resort and for the next few decades built it into one of the most popular of its time along with the Red, White, Sweet and Hot Springs.

They operated a store at the springs and built cabins and a frame hotel. The large stone hotel which is still standing today as a private residence was built between 1820 and 1825. People from all over the South began flocking to the spa for both health and social reasons. The resort was especially popular with South Carolinians, and they even had a row of cottages appropriately named "Nullification Row."

The increased number of guests in the early 1830s made the owners, Erskine and Caruthers, so confident that about 1836 they constructed the elegant Erskine House on a ridge above the valley. It was 206 by 45 feet and contained 72 rooms. Next to the house they built a number of brick cottages, two of which remain today. Only some stone and the foundations are left from the Erskine House, however.

During the Civil War the resort was used as a rest area and headquarters by both armies. Apparently there was not much damage to the buildings, but only meager maintenance work was done. Erskine's wife ran the place as best she could under the wartime restrictions. Her husband had died in 1863.

After the war the resort remained closed until 1867 when the Salt Sulphur Springs Com-

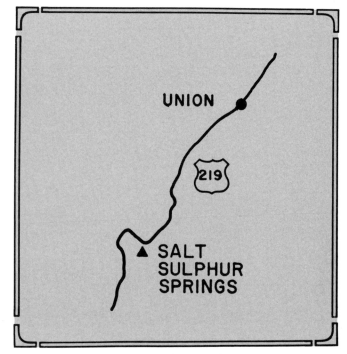

pany was formed with Adam King, of Washington, D.C., as president. There is no record of the resort being operated again until 1882, although camp meetings had been held in the 1870s. When Col. J.W.M. Appleton became manager in 1882, the resort was upgraded considerably and regained some of its past glory.

But by the turn of the century the business had begun to deteriorate, and after Appleton died in 1913, the springs closed. The property was sold at public auction in 1918, and in 1922 it was again sold to P.E. Holz of Charleston, West Virginia. Holz made improvements and reopened the spa, but the business failed to make a comeback. Social conditions were much different in the depression years, and in 1936 the resort closed for good.

The present owner is Mrs. Ward Wylie who along with her late husband bought the resort in the 1960s, restored the stone hotel as a private residence, and also restored the two brick cottages and two stone spring houses on the property.

Beyer's rendering of Salt Sulphur Springs from his 1857 Album of Virginia.   VA

The Erskine House in the early 1900s. It was the last large building built at the resort in the late 1830s and contained 72 rooms.

Dr. Margaret Ballard
Union, W. Va.

-159-

Dining room in the main hotel in 1963.   VA

Registration desk in the main hotel in 1963 before the building was restored.   VA

An early view of the springs.

Ballroom in the main hotel in 1963.   VA

The main hotel built in the 1820s and restored in the 1960s as a private residence.

Ruins of the Erskine House, which started to deteriorate rapidly in the 1940s.

Restored brick cottages at the springs. VA

The bath house, spring house and original store from the 1820s.

Sweet Springs

Located close to the junction of S.R. 3 and 311 at the western tip of Monroe County on the Virginia border.

Of all the surviving pre-Civil War spas in West Virginia or Virginia, Sweet Springs is perhaps the most spectacular. Approaching the resort site from either state route, one sees ahead a large Georgian Colonial structure said to have been designed by Thomas Jefferson.

As for the spa's history, James Mons was the first settler in about 1764, and William Lewis began developing the area as a resort not long after the Revolutionary War. He built the first hotel in 1792 which makes Sweet Springs one of the oldest spas along with Berkeley and Warm Springs.

District court proceedings for the counties of Botetourt, Greenbrier, Kanawha and Montgomery were held here for eleven years until being moved to Lewisburg in Greenbrier County in 1807.

The spring water has been described as the best acidulous water in the United States. It contains quite a lot of carbonic acid (fixed air) which gives it a peculiar briskness. For many years the spring water was credited with remarkable cures of sub-acute rheumatism and neuralgia. Immersions in the water were also recommended to relieve nephritic complaints. The springs are thermal and are similar to the famous springs of Bristol, England.

Lewis went on to envision a town to be called Fontville, which would be a health resort, but the public showed no interest in investing in the project. Despite this failure, the resort prospered. Thomas Jefferson was employed to design a new resort complex, and his plans called for the construction of a circle of buildings around the springs. But, only the Jefferson Building, three two-story guest homes and the Ball Building were ever built, all of them of brick. Many frame structures were built for slaves and livery and main-

tenance purposes. Most of these were built in 1833, long after Jefferson's death, and it is not known how well his plans were followed.

The brick buildings are still intact today. The Jefferson Building is the main home for the aged, and the Ball Building just to the north was used as a women's residence until recently. The cottages are still in use, and the bath house, built at the same time as the other buildings, could be used again if some clean up work were done.

The elegance of Sweet Springs drew hundreds of guests and many well-known ones. General Lafayette, President and Mrs. George Washington, Chief Justice John Marshall, Patrick Henry, General Robert E. Lee, James and Dolley Madison and Presidents Millard Fillmore and Franklin Pierce all visited here.

During the Civil War, armies passed through the valley and undoubtedly used the resort facilities, but fortunately they did no damage. After the war, the resort continued to

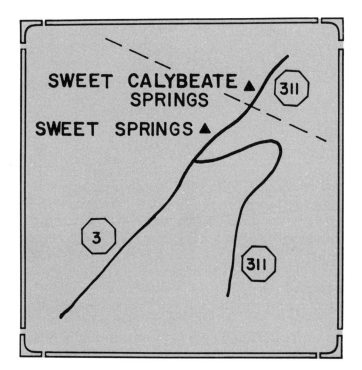

operate, but certainly not with the same gaiety it once had.

The coming of the railroad in the 1870s made it easier to get to the spa. The hotel at that time could hold 800 guests.

In 1852 the property had passed out of the hands of the Lewis family and from then on many managers and owners were involved in the operation until the late 1920s when it finally went into receivership.

Mons Taylor, a wealthy man from Roanoke purchased the resort in 1930, but it turned out to be a financial liability, and he sold it to the State of West Virginia in 1945. It was used first as a tuberculosis sanatorium and later turned into the Andrew S. Rowan Memorial Home for the Aged. In 1972 construction began on a fourth portico to the old Jefferson Hotel. Today the building stands as a reminder of the dozens of health spas that were such an important part of the history of the two states.

Beyer's rendering of Sweet Springs from his 1857 Album of Virginia.   VA

The magnificent old Sweet Springs hotel, built in 1833 and now used as a state home for the aged. The left part of the building is new.

One of several original brick cottages still in use. They were built in the 1830s.
Sweet Springs hotel in the stagecoach days.   VA

The old bath house and pool—still in good condition.

Bath house constructed in the 1830s. VA

The Ball Building, originally built as a ballroom and at one time was considered one of the three largest and most beautiful in the Old South. It was converted into a women's residence hall but is no longer used.

Webster Springs

Located at the town of Webster Springs, Webster County.

Fork Lick, so named because there was a salt lick where the Elk River forks, was used by Indians long before white settlers came into the region. Herds of elk, deer and buffalo beat down trails to the salt sulphur springs that oozed from the bank of the river.

A post office was established near the spring in 1852, and later the name was changed to Webster Courthouse, then Addison, and finally to Webster Springs in 1902.

During the Civil War, Union troops filled up the old salt well and broke up the kettles used in making salt from the springs. They also burned down most of the buildings in the town.

Senator Johnson N. Camden and B&O Railroad interests built a hotel near the springs in 1897. In 1902 a railroad was built to the town, and this started a 15-year building boom. Thirty-one hotels are thought to have existed in the town at one time or another, and on October 1, 1902 the Webster Springs Sanitarium Company was chartered to construct a hospital, hotel and electric plant.

John T. McGraw bought the hotel in 1903 and renovated and greatly expanded it to 300 rooms, 75 with bath. It was the largest frame building in West Virginia and the second largest hotel in the state. It was equipped with Turkish and Russian baths and was very elegant for the rather isolated community. A stone and frame spring enclosure was built over the Salt Sulphur Springs well and the water was bottled and shipped around the country.

Business dropped off considerably during World War I, and the hotel closed its doors in 1920. McGraw died that year, and the resort changed hands a number of times. Several tries were made to bring the business back, but it never again operated profitably.

Then on July 20, 1925, the magnificent hotel burned to the ground, with arson suspected as the cause. Seventeen guests escaped with their belongings. Several days later the 27 acres of property were sold as lots.

Salt brine wells and the Webster Springs Hotel around 1900.

William Gillespie
Charleston, W. Va.

The 300 room Webster Springs Hotel about 1908. It was the largest frame structure and the second largest hotel in the state at this time.
West Virginia University Archives

Enclosure over the Salt Sulphur Springs well after John McGraw renovated in about 1906.
West Virginia University Archives

White Sulphur Springs

Located on the west edge of White Sulphur Springs, Greenbrier County.

The White is the one resort which all others are compared to. It was and is the largest that was spawned by mineral waters in the Virginias and is one of the premier resorts in the United States today.

It all started back around 1750 when Nicholas and Kate Carpenter settled on Howard's Creek. They built a small log home and lived there with their infant daughter, Frances. Then in 1752 Nicholas was killed in an Indian raid. Kate saved herself and her baby by hiding an entire day and night in the thick forest of a mountain, since called Kate's Mountain, to the east of the Springs. Mother and child eventually moved to Staunton, and in 1766 Frances married Michael Bowyer, a prominent local soldier and statesman.

Acquiring title to land that Frances had inherited and adding to it purchases of his own, Bowyer became the owner of the nucleus of the future resort property and moved there in the 1780s. People were already squatting on the land and using the mineral waters.

One of Bowyer's daughters, Mary, married James Calwell, and when Bowyer died in 1809, the Calwells inherited the property. They built a small tavern near the Springs, and this was the beginning of the world-famous resort. The Lester Building, now used as an employees' dormitory, is one of the oldest structures still standing, and the spring enclosure dates back to about 1815.

The Alabama, Louisiana, Paradise and Baltimore rows or cottages were built in the first few decades of the nineteenth century, and the present President's Cottage, built in 1834, was the first of the grand private cottages. Stephen Henderson, a wealthy sugar planter from New Orleans, had it built for his use and after his death, many presidents made it their summer White House and it became known as the President's Cottage.

Henry Clay in 1817 was one of the first prominent Americans to frequent the growing spa, and it might be said that he set a precedent for the annual trek to the resort that has occurred since.

Construction in 1824 of the James River and Kanawha Turnpike, alongside the spa, really stimulated business. People could take a stagecoach or ride horseback from eastern Virginia, or they could take a boat up the Mississippi and Ohio rivers to the Virginia border and then travel on the new road, 150 miles to the spa.

Guests flocked to White Sulphur in the mid 1800s, as it became the "in" place to go during the summer season. President Andrew Jackson may have encouraged this trend; as he was the first president known to have stayed at the resort. Many others followed through the years.

During the financial panic of 1837, President Martin Van Buren and his advisors used

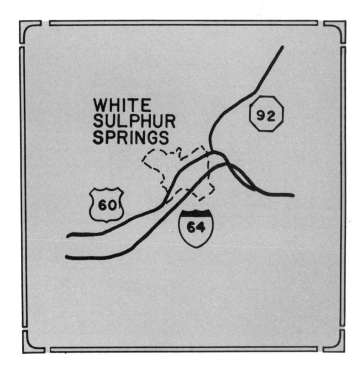

the resort as a summer White House and worked there on politics to bring the country out of the crisis.

Calwell, the owner, who was held in high regard by his guests, had done a great job of developing his spa, but had borrowed heavily to do so. He borrowed $20,000 in 1817, which he was unable to repay, and continued to borrow until, at the time of his death in 1851, he was in debt for more than $400,000.

His son took over the resort and incorporated the White Sulphur Springs Company. He began construction of a huge hotel which his father had left plans for, but he could not sell enough stock to keep the business going. In the spring of 1857 the property was sold to a group of Virginia men who continued construction of the hotel. It opened in 1858 as the largest hotel in the United States. It was 400 feet square with a dining room that could seat 1,200. At first it was called "Grand Central Hotel," but later came to be known as "Old White."

When Greenbrier County voted for secession in 1861, most of the men in the county joined the new Confederate Army. During the war the resort was occupied by both sides. A major battle in West Virginia was fought just east of the spa on August 26, 1863. Confederate troops under the command of Colonel George Patton, grandfather of the famous World War II general, George Patton, Jr., held off Union forces under General William Averell.

On June 25, 1864 the resort came close to being destroyed. General David Hunter, occupying it, decided to burn it down. Captain Henry duPont, his chief of artillery, persuaded him not to in case the Union Army would pass this way again and would again need the facilities. Thus the argument of one man saved the resort.

A railroad to bring guests to the spa from the east and west had been discussed and dreamed of for years. In 1869 the dreams began to come true when the tracks were laid from the east to White Sulphur Springs. Soon the trains arrived, and many years of prosperity followed. General Robert E. Lee spent much time at the spa in the late 1860s, and this further enhanced its popularity.

George Peyton and his brothers had leased the resort after the war, but subsequently William Stuart, a wealthy farmer and salt baron, foreclosed on them and formed the Greenbrier White Sulphur Springs Company in 1882. He built a large wing on the "Old White," a race track and other improvements. Then Grover Dulany foreclosed on Stuart in 1888 and took over the operation.

Golf and White Sulphur Springs have been synonymous for years. The first golf club in America was organized near here in 1884, and the first tournament was held in 1887.

Beyer's rendering of White Sulphur Springs from his 1857 Album of Virginia. VA

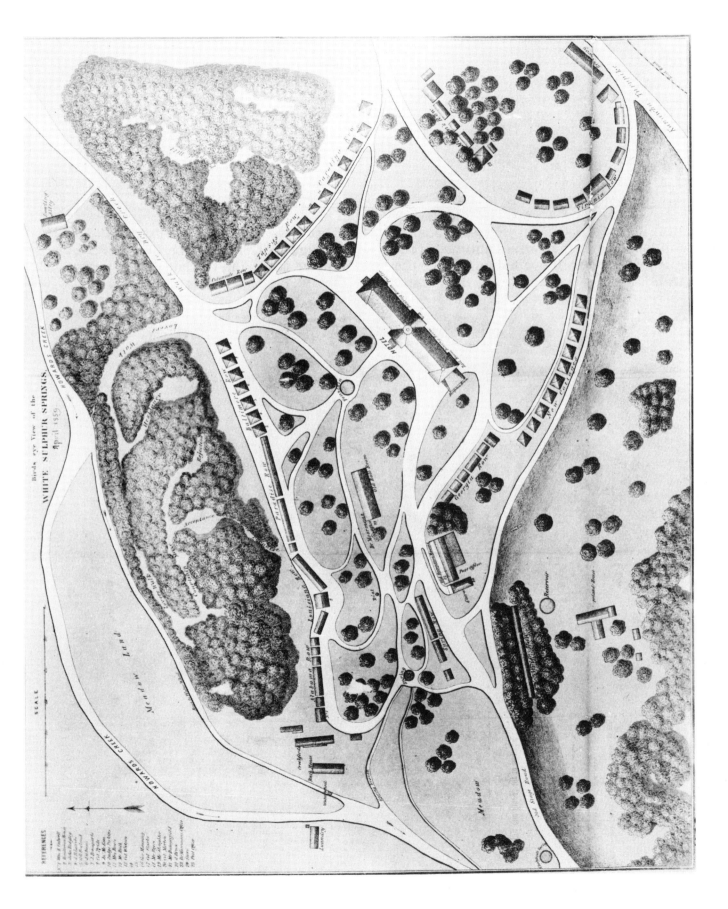

White Sulphur Springs in 1859.

The Greenbrier

(The first course was opened at the resort in 1910).

The purchase of the property in 1910 by the Chesapeake and Ohio Railway signaled a new period of improvements and prosperity. In 1913 construction of the Greenbrier Hotel was completed (it is the center section of the present hotel) with 225 rooms on seven floors. The Georgian style design is by Frederick Junius Sterner, a well-known New York architect. An indoor pool was built in 1912, an 18-hole golf course in 1914 and golf club house in 1916. Tennis courts also were added.

The Old White and the Greenbrier hotels were operated separately until 1922 when the Old White was finally torn down because it could not meet the fire codes. In 1931, the railroad spent over three million dollars to expand the hotel to 580 rooms. An auditorium was added, and all the cottages were renovated.

Business continued through the Depression years and an airport was built in 1930. The resort boasted of 7,000 acres and was hailed as "America's Most Beautiful All-Year Resort."

Right after Pearl Harbor, Japanese, German and Hungarian diplomats were interned at the hotel. After they were exchanged for American diplomats in July 1942, the hotel reopened to the public. However, in September the U.S. Army purchased the spa for three million dollars and converted it to the Ashford General Hospital. It could house 2,200 patients, and more than 20,000 were treated here during the war.

At the end of the war, the railroad repurchased the property for three million, three hundred thousand dollars and held a gala party in April 1948, to celebrate the reopening.

Many improvements and additions have been made since then—the West Wing in 1954, the West Virginia Wing in 1962, a conference complex in 1974, the new golf club

WHITE SULPHUR SPRINGS, WEST VIRGINIA.

White Sulphur Springs and the "Old White" in the 1880s.   The Greenbrier

building in 1976, a new pool, tennis courts and golf courses.

White Sulphur Springs is truly a year-round resort with many attractions. It is a lasting tribute to Bowyer, Calwell, Dr. John Moorman, the resident physician for nearly 50 years, and others who made a dream come true.

"Old White" in the 1880s. Facade to the left was the main entrance. It was torn down in 1922 as it could not meet the fire codes.
The Greenbrier

The archway connecting the Greenbrier Hotel to the right and the "Old White." It stood from 1913 to 1922. The area is now the North entrance.
The Greenbrier

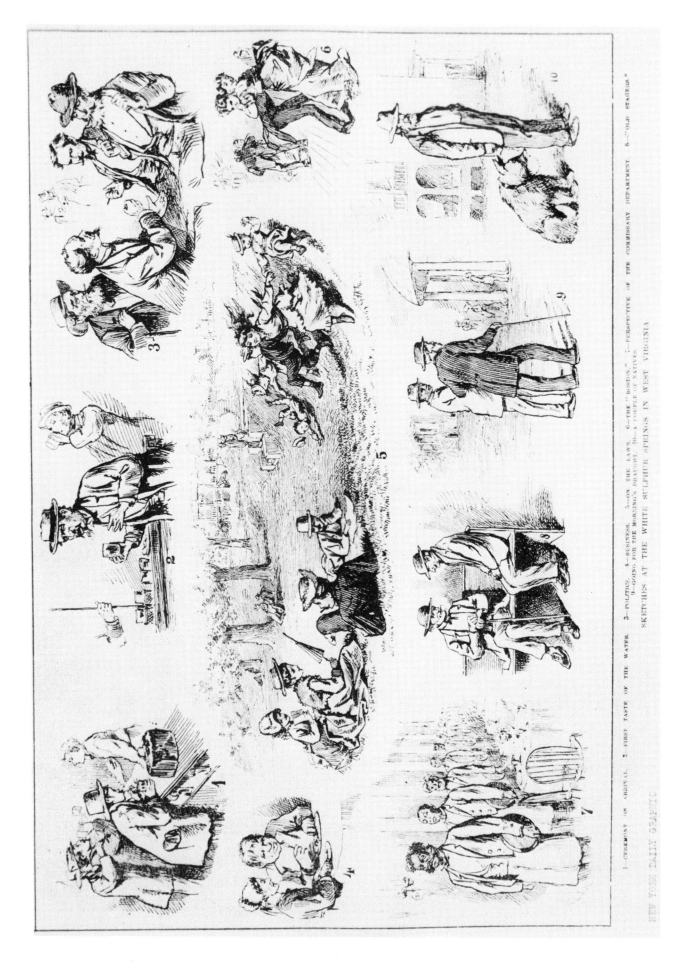

1.—CEREMONY OF ARRIVAL. 2.—FIRST TASTE OF THE WATER. 3.—POLITICS. 4.—BUSINESS. 5.—ON THE LAWN. 6.—THE "BOSTON." 7.—PERSPECTIVE OF THE COMMISSARY DEPARTMENT. 8.—"OLD STAGERS." 9.—GOING FOR THE MORNING'S DRAUGHT. 10.—A COUPLE OF NATIVES.

SKETCHES AT THE WHITE SULPHUR SPRINGS IN WEST VIRGINIA

NEW YORK DAILY GRAPHIC

WHITE SULPHUR SPRINGS
WEST VIRGINIA
SINCE 1778

Table d'Hote Luncheon

Clam Chowder Manhattan
OR
Cold Essence of Tomatoes

———

Grilled Fresh Mackerel, Anchovy Butter
OR
Egg Stuffed with Caviar

———

Chicken Patty a la Reine
OR
Roast Prime Beef au Jus
OR
Cold Spring Lamb with Vegetable Salad

———

Scalloped Fresh Tomatoes   Steamed Rice
Baked or Saute Potatoes

———

Lettuce with French Dressing

———

Old Fashion Bread Pudding or Fresh Peach

———

(Choice of One)

Tea   Coffee   Milk   Buttermilk

Sweet Cider per glass 20   Friday, August 19, 1921

Served from 12.30 to 2.15 P. M.

The Greenbrier Hotel in 1929. The ornate pedestals on top of the building have been removed.

The Greenbrier

A group of guests at the Springs, 1887. The Greenbrier

On the veranda of the "Bruce Cottage" in August 1908. From left to right: Major General Clarence Edwards, commander of the Rainbow Division in World War I; Mrs. William H. Taft; Joseph Holt Gaines, Member of Congress; William H. Taft, President of the United States, 1909-1913; and Mrs. Joseph H. Gaines. The Greenbrier

General Robert E. Lee and friends at the Springs in 1869. According to the now accepted identifications, subjects seated in the photograph, commencing from the left, are 1) Blacque Bey, Turkish Minister to the United States, 1867 to 1873; 2) General Lee; 3) George Peabody of Massachusetts, philanthropist; 4) W.W. Corcoran of Washington, philanthropist, donor of the Corcoran Gallery; 5) Judge James Lyons of Richmond, Va., lawyer, member of the House of Representatives in the First Confederate Congress., 1862-4. All subjects standing are Confederate Generals. Commencing from the left, 1) General James Conner of South Carolina, attorney general of that State under Wade Hampton; 2) General Martin W. Gary of South Carolina; 3) Major General J. Bankhead Magruder of Virginia; 4) General Robert D. Lilley of Virginia; 5) General Beauregard of Louisiana; 6) General Alexander R. Lawton of Georgia; 7) General Henry A. Wise of Virginia, Governor of Virginia during the period of John Brown's raid; 8) General Joseph L. Brent of Maryland, who died in 1905, last survivor of all Americans in the photograph.

The Greenbrier

The Old White ball at the Greenbrier in the 1930s.

The Greenbrier

Mrs. Woodrow Wilson unveiling a portrait of General Lee at the Lee Week Ball in 1932.

The Greenbrier

The Greenbrier – White Sulphur Springs, W. Va.

The Greenbrier Hotel as it appeared in the 1940s.

North facade of the Greenbrier in 1940.

NORTH FACADE   THE GREENBRIER HOTEL   WHITE SULPHUR SPRINGS W. VA.

An elevator shaft built on the outside of the ballroom during World War II when the hotel was used as a hospital. The shaft was demolished after the C and O bought the hotel back in 1946.

The Greenbrier

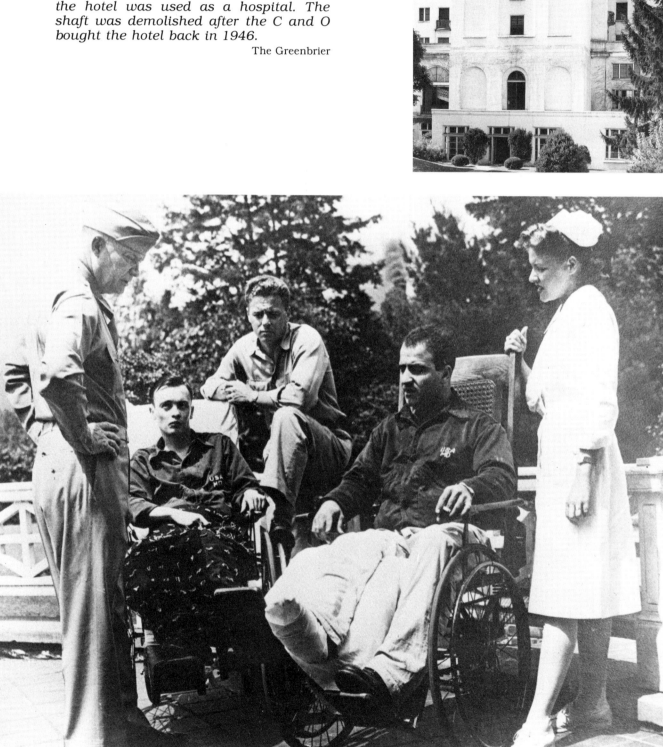

General Dwight Eisenhower visiting the Ashford General Hospital, as the hotel was called then, in 1945.

The Greenbrier

The spring house at White Sulphur Springs, built about 1815. The statue of hygeia on top was donated by Stephen Henderson who built the President's Cottage. The original statue was destroyed during the Civil War. The Greenbrier

North entrance to the Greenbrier Hotel.
The Greenbrier

The Prince of Wales, later the Duke of Windsor, at the Greenbrier in 1919.
The Greenbrier

The President's Cottage, built in 1834, by a wealthy New Orleans planter. Now a museum.

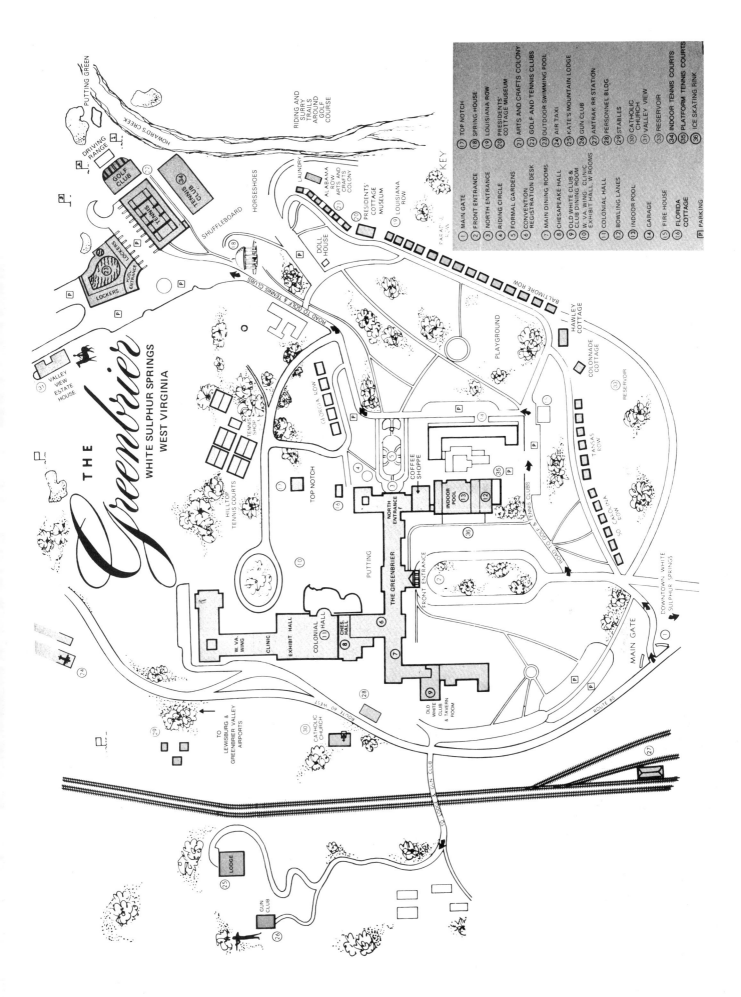

THE *Greenbrier*
WHITE SULPHUR SPRINGS
WEST VIRGINIA

KEY

1 MAIN GATE
2 FRONT ENTRANCE
3 NORTH ENTRANCE
4 RIDING CIRCLE
5 FORMAL GARDENS
6 CONVENTION REGISTRATION DESK
7 MAIN DINING ROOMS
8 CHESAPEAKE HALL
9 OLD WHITE CLUB & CLUB DINING ROOM
10 W. VA. WING: CLINIC, EXHIBIT HALL, W ROOMS
11 COLONIAL HALL
12 BOWLING LANES
13 INDOOR POOL
14 GARAGE
15 FIRE HOUSE
16 FLORIDA COTTAGE
P PARKING

17 TOP NOTCH
18 SPRING HOUSE
19 LOUISIANA ROW
20 PRESIDENTS COTTAGE MUSEUM
21 ARTS AND CRAFTS COLONY
22 GOLF AND TENNIS CLUBS
23 OUTDOOR SWIMMING POOL
24 AIR TAXI
25 KATE'S MOUNTAIN LODGE
26 GUN CLUB
27 AMTRAK RR STATION
28 PERSONNEL BLDG.
29 STABLES
30 CATHOLIC CHURCH
31 VALLEY VIEW
33 RESERVOIR
34 INDOOR TENNIS COURTS
35 PLATFORM TENNIS COURTS
36 ICE SKATING RINK

GRAND BALL MASQUE,

, AT THE

White Sulphur Springs,

AUGUST 27, 1868.

～～～～～～～～

FLOOR COMMITTEE.

Dr. J. HANSON THOMAS,
Mr. JOHN ANDREWS,
Judge SAM'L J. DOUGLAS,
Mr. DOUGLASS TAYLOR,
Mr. RICHARD H. SPENCER,
Mr. J. T. PERKINS,
Col. B. C. ADAMS,
Mr. L. H. SERGENT.

To avoid confusion, parties will engage "vis-a-vis" beforehand.

Independent. pr. Lewisburg.

Other Springs

Bennett Springs

Located at the junction of C.R. 740 and C.R. 912, five miles north of Salem, Roanoke County.

George Bennett discovered the springs in 1889 while horseback riding through the country. He envisioned a resort and persuaded 30 people from Roanoke to invest in the Bennett Springs Corporation. The group bought a hundred and sixty acres, and members drew lots to see where they would build their summer cottages.

This private resort was for corporation members only and they built a swimming pool and tennis courts in addition to their cottages. For years members enjoyed picnics and family get-togethers, but by the late 1970s most of the original families were gone, and the area was sold to outsiders. Some of the original cabins still remain.

Black Rock Springs

Located within the borders of Shenandoah National Park in the extreme northeastern corner of Augusta County near Still Run, approximately 20 miles from Staunton.

The resort was bought by some people from New York in the late 1850s and renamed Union Springs. This turned out to be a poor name for a resort catering to southerners, especially just before the Civil War. Business dropped off before the war and completely during the war. It was sold at auction in June 1869 in a bad state of repair.

Before the turn of the century a hotel and 28 cottages were built, but along with stables and barns, they all were destroyed by fire on November 4, 1909.

Bloomer Springs

Located on the east side of Massanutten mountain, four miles south of Elkton, Rockingham County.

Bloomer Springs opened in 1852 as a small health resort, and about a dozen cottages were built and used by local people. The name was chosen because of the "blooms" made at a nearby iron furnace.

Blue Healing Springs

Located four miles west of Craig Healing Springs on S.R. 658.

One building still remains on the north side of the road. It was the ballroom and later served as a hunting lodge. A golf course was reportedly built north of the ballroom. A man in Florida now owns this overgrown former spa.

Blue Sulphur Springs

Located near Barboursville, Cabell County, West Virginia near the Mud River.

West Virginia had two Blue Sulphur Springs, one in Greenbrier and another, a little known resort, in Cabell County.

Several springs were discovered in the latter area, and on July 4, 1885, George Floding opened a hotel consisting of three stories and 35 rooms. The site had been known as Floding Springs, but, perhaps for advertising purposes, the name was changed to Blue Sulphur Springs. Guests could take the train from Huntington nine miles west or travel on the old James River and Kanawha Turnpike.

From time to time Floding hired managers and caretakers to operate the spa. James Edward McDowell took over the management in the early 1900s, but by 1910 the hotel had to close because of a lack of business.

New owners reopened the spa about 1922, but the aura of the past was gone, and later the hotel was torn down. There is no mention of any other structure at the small resort.

Brunswick Inn Lithia Springs

Located in Waynesboro, Augusta County at 13th Street and Wayne Avenue.

A lithia spring at this site prompted the Newell Brothers to build a hotel there in 1891. It was called the Brunswick Hotel, and society people from Richmond flocked to it for many years. The name was changed to Ford's Hotel in 1899 and later to the Brunswick Inn.

Dupont Chemical Company leased the building from 1929 to 1932 to house employees who were building a local chemical plant. The inn was closed in 1937, and now all traces of the hotel and the springs are gone.

Chase City Mineral Springs

Located in Chase City, Mecklenburg, County.

Another spring in the county, similar to Buffalo, was located at Chase City. Some years after the Civil War, the popularity of the area increased and several hotels were built in town to take care of the visitors. In 1903, the Chase City Mineral Water Company built the famous Mecklenburg Hotel and bottling house. The hotel had 150 rooms and stood atop a gentle hill. It was very fashionable and had extensive facilities. People from all over the country flocked here for the hotel accommodations and the water. But six years later, it all ended when the hotel burned to the ground.

Several attempts were made to establish a new company to carry on the traditions, but in 1927 the property was subdivided into house lots and nothing remains today.

Cluster Springs

Located six miles from South Boston on Route 501 South, Halifax Country. Indians and early day settlers frequented the area where there was a cluster of springs. In the 1830s Dr. Henry Easley began to develop the springs into a resort with a hotel, tavern and stables. The resort flourished until the Civil War forced it to close. At the close of the war the springs was purchased by Dr. John Shearer for the purpose of opening a boys' school. Various people operated a school at Cluster Springs and in 1893 a modern boys' school was established and additional buildings were constructed. The school became well known and drew students from many surrounding states. Cluster Springs Academy operated until 1917 when World War I forced its closing for good. Only one original building--the Ryburn Cottage--still remains from the resort era. The rest of the area is largely overgrown.

Daggers Springs

Located in the extreme northwest part of Botetount County on the main road between Lynchburg and White Sulphur Springs and at the base of the Garden Mountain.

This resort first opened for business before 1820, operated by a man named Dagger. It was then bought by James Dibrell of Richmond and in 1859 by a Mr. Houston and a Mr. Shields. A hotel for 200 guests was built, most of these guests coming from the surrounding area. The spring water was sulphurous and similar to White Sulphur Springs.

Gray Sulphur Springs

This remote, little known resort was located 3/4 mile from Peterstown, West Virginia just over the Virginia border in Giles County. It reportedly opened in 1831, and in 1833 could boast of a brick hotel 90 feet by 32 feet with accommodations for over 100 people and two tiers of cabins for additional 80 to 10 people. A stage ran three days a week to Red, Salt and White Sulphur Springs. No other mention could be found of this resort, and no trace remains of it today. It seems to have disappeared into complete oblivion.

Grayson Sulphur Springs

This little known resort operated for more than 75 years. It was located on the north bank of the New River, about 20 miles from Wytheville in Carroll County between Fries and Byllsby. It was first recorded as a health resort in 1835 when it was organized by a group of county citizens. In the 1840s a large two-story building and many cottages were constructed. The area was very mountainous and only the springs along the river bank were level. In 1859 a flood caused severe damage and the Civil War closed the area for many years. The resort would not open again until 1886 and a new hotel, the Riverside Inn was built in 1897. In 1913 the property was purchased by the New River Power Company and with the construction of a dam at Byllsby, the resort was inundated.

Green Sulphur Springs

Located on S.R. 20, 15 miles north of Hinton, Summers County, West Virginia.

Although it was never a resort per se like other nearby sites, its water has been visited ever since a well was drilled there in 1818, and for years the bottled water was shipped throughout the country.

The property has been in the Gwinn family

since 1779. In 1818 a drill was brought on muleback from Cincinnati to the farm, and a well was drilled 65 feet deep. Ephriam Gwinn had found the sulphur spring when he discovered that wild aminals pawed and licked the earth at a low damp spot.

In the mid 1800s, Green Sulphur water was a thriving business. A statement by chemical analysis contained this information:

"Green Sulphur water, a great tonic mineral water unexcelled in the treatment of stomach, bladder and kidney diseases, makes you feel like a new man. Nature's tonic comes from an artesian well...Drink the water freely; one or two glasses early in the morning, and before each meal. This water can be drunk in any reasonable quantity with good effect."

Hopkins Springs

Located on the east side of Massanutten Mountain, five miles south of Elkton, Rockingham County.

This spa was developed around 1870 by G.T. Hopkins and his son, Edwin. They named the resort the Rockingham Virginia Mineral Springs. By 1874 facilities included a two-story, forty-room hotel, two other guest houses—the Pine Cottage and the Baltimore House, a bowling alley and a laundry.

In 1879, the well-known American poet Sidney Lanier spent the summer here and finished his notable book, *The Science of English Verse*, "in the quiet and shade of the mountains."

A three-story hotel was constructed in 1893. All the buildings were torn down after World War I, and today the Massanutten Village development occupies the site.

Jordan Alum Springs

Located next to Rockbridge Alum Springs.

Capitalizing on spa traffic in the area, John W. Jordan, who owned 500 acres adjoining the Rockbridge Alum Springs, built his own resort. The Jordan Alum Company purchased the site in 1872, at which time there was a three-story hotel, 105 by 136 feet, and detached cottages. Each hotel room had an electric bell for calling the office, and each floor had gas lights and a water closet.

From 1872 until 1880 there was bitter litigation between the Jordan and Rockbridge Alums. A high board fence was erected between the properties, which were only a few hundred feet apart. Then Jordan's advertisements stated that a skilled gymnast could vault the fence. Rockbridge would not permit visits from Jordan guests, and Jordan would not allow Rockbridge guests to attend its dances. Employees of the two resorts often engaged in fist fights.

In 1880 the controversy was resolved. The fence was removed and a covered board walk was built to connect the hotels. The two finally merged sometime in the 1880s and the Jordan property became the most popular resort.

Johnston's Springs

Located on the west end of Salem, Roanoke County.

Joe Chapman, a prominent hotel man of the Roanoke area in the 1870s, opened his Lake Spring Hotel at the old Johnston's Springs site in 1876. The hotel would accommodate 150 guests, and he brought to it not only the Salem town band but also an Italian string band.

The enterprising hotel man shipped water from this spring and from Roanoke Red Sulphur Springs, which he also owned.

The hotel subsequently burned down.

Kimberling Springs

Located in Bland County north of Wytheville.

In its day this spa was very popular in this section of southwest Virginia.

A hotel was built about 1854 by Edwin S. Booth of New York. The main building was a three-story frame structure. As many as 500 guests could be accommodated when the hotel was at its prime. In the early 1860s, the spa was managed by a couple from Bluefield in what was to become West Virginia.

The resort was famous for its dances, race course and medieval tournaments. Visitors came from all parts of the south for these tournaments.

For 26 years the resort was in use, but it closed in 1880 and lumber from its buildings went to many buildings in the county. An annual picnic was held at the site in the 1930s and 40s.

Liberty Springs

Located north of Rawley Springs, in Rockingham County.

The Liberty Springs Company bought 52 acres in 1845 for $32. In 1857 the company bought an additional 158 acres for $100. Cabins were built here prior to the Civil War but were burned down during the war to keep would-be Confederate Army draft dodgers and deserters from living in them. By 1911, some 20 cabins were rebuilt, but rough roads precluded any further development.

Mercer Healing Springs

Mercer Healing Springs is located on Gardner Road between the West Virginia Turnpike and State Route 20 in Mercer County, West Virginia, approximately one-half mile from the Concord College exit. The spring was discovered sometime between 1870 and 1880. Around 1900, with the development of the vast coal fields in the area, the Mercer Healing Springs Corporation was formed to develop a resort. A springhouse, cottages and a hotel were constructed. In 1908 Rufus Meador bought the resort and constructed a new 65-room hotel. Visitors were brought within four miles of the resort to Princeton by the Virginian Railroad.

The water was, and still is, clear, colorless, odorless and has only a slight mineral taste. It was reported to be Alkaline-Calcic-Chalybeate and was good for the skin, kidneys and bowels. This water was bottled and shipped throughout the United States.

Meador operated the hotel until 1920 when he sold it to two Princeton doctors. The large hotel burned down in 1922 and this put an end to the resort business. A large frame house now sits on the site of the old hotel building and the present owners have built a springhouse over the original spring.

Millboro Springs

Located two miles from the Millboro Station of the C and O Railroad in Bath County.

A way station was located here in the 1790s, and a tavern in the 1830s. A 100-guest hotel was built a few years before the Civil War. The Virginia Central Railroad, the forerunner of the C and O, reached Millboro in 1856 and the resort flourished afterward.

Apparently it was in operation until World War I. Then in 1935, E.J. Wimmer bought the vacant hotel. All structures were burned down, and a new road was built over the resort site.

Mountain Top Hotel & Springs

Located three miles east of Waynesboro, Augusta County, just below the entrance to the Swannanoa Country Club at the Rockfish Gap of the Blue Ridge Mountains.

The Mountain Top Inn was a popular hotel and resort and a favorite stopover for travelers going from the east across the Shenandoah Valley to the summer resorts in the Alleghenies. It was first built in 1770 and known as Rockfish Inn. Freestone and chalybeate springs were found in the area.

The old inn became famous after an important conference was held there in 1818. Twenty one Virginia citizens, including Jefferson, Madison and Monroe, met to choose the location for a proposed state university.

The inn was originally built of stone, and it was upgraded considerably through the years. Gen. Lee spent the night here on Sept. 17, 1865 when he was on his way to assume the presidency of Washington College in Lexington.

On April 4, 1909, the hotel was destroyed by fire, and the site is now covered over by Interstate 64.

Patrick Springs

Located at Patrick Springs, Patrick County, on U.S. 58 above the North Carolina border.

This was an academy for women before it was a spa. It reached its peak after the Civil War, with George Washington Morrison as its colorful manager. The resort stayed open until the start of World War II, and in 1954 its four-story hotel burned to the ground.

Shannondale Springs

Located 5 1/2 miles south of Charles Town, Jefferson County, West Virginia, on a peninsula of the Shenandoah River called the "Horse Shoe."

George Washington is reported to have used these waters when he was surveying part of Lord Fairfax's land grant. Then in 1819 a large brick hotel and 10 or 12 smaller buildings were erected. There were three springs—red, white and blue—but only the white, with a constant 55° temperature, was used.

Many famous people came to the resort including James Monroe, Andrew Jackson, Martin Van Buren, Millard Fillmore and John C. Calhoun.

Fire destroyed the fashionable buildings in 1858, but some were rebuilt, and Presidents Hayes, Garfield and Arthur used Shannondale as an unofficial summer White House in the late 19th Century. In 1909 another disastrous fire struck the resort, and it never recovered. Today the resort is the site of a housing subdivision.

Shenandoah Alum Springs

Located 2 1/2 miles north of Orkney Springs on C.R. 717 and 12 miles west of Mt. Jackson, Shenandoah County.

This was a popular resort in the 1870s along with Orkney Springs. The resort was owned by A.J. Myers, and at one time a post office was here, and an old iron furnace was on Stony Creek. Nothing remains today.

Sparkling Springs

Located at the base of Little North Mountain, two miles west of Singers Glen, Rockingham County.

The Sparkling Springs Company bought 120 acres including the springs (originally called Baxter Spring) in 1886. Mineral content of the springs included iron, magnesia and sulphur.

The company built two-story cottages in the deep ravine where the spring house was located. In 1899 a charter was issued to the Springs company which boasted a capital stock of $5,000.

In addition to the cottages, a boarding house, dairy and croquet grounds were constructed, and in 1930 electricity was brought in. Through the years cabins have continued to be built, and the site remains a pleasant mountain retreat.

Union Springs

Located five miles south of Rawley Springs on Narrow Back Mountain in Rockingham County.

Local people from this part of the country built summer cottages in this area, and several of them took in visitors. There was never a hotel built. New cabins are located today at the old springs site.

Variety Springs

Located 15 miles west of Staunton, Augusta County at Pond Gap.

The resort, also known as Mt. Elliot Springs, contained alum, chalybeate and freestone waters. The resort, which was built before the Civil War, had a 200-guest hotel, cottages and plunge baths. It was on the Virginia Central, later the C&O Railroad line.

A newspaper account states that in 1879 and again in 1887 the resort was sold at auction.

According to a later news story, a swimming pool was built and other improvements were made in 1901. No record when the resort closed could be found.

Wyrick Springs

Located one mile south of Crockett, Wythe County on State Route 625. Named for E.R. Wyrick who purchased the site in 1876. While building a fence around the largely swampy ground, he accidently opened up the spring and after draining the swamp, a beautiful area emerged. By 1900 Wyrick and a partner had made some developments at the area for bathers and the bottling of the water. M.S. Bennett bought the area in 1911 and built a thirty-room hotel and store. For many years the resort was operated by several owners and was popular with visitors from a wide area. The bottled water was shipped throughout the east. By 1935 the hotel was closed and rented out as a private residence. It was finally dismantled in 1957.

Virginia Mineral Springs

Located on C.R. 615, three miles north of

New Castle, Craig County.

This small resort was a direct result of the iron ore boom in Craig County in the late 1890s and early 1900s. A railroad was built into New Castle, the county seat, to handle the anticipated shipment of the ore. New Castle boomed and two big hotels were built to handle the expected visitors—the Bel Air on the hill above the town and the Craig City Inn to the east. When it was discovered that the cost of mining the ore was prohibitive, the boom was suddenly over.

In 1912, the Graham, Reynolds, Lee Company moved the four-story Craig City Inn three miles north to a site known as Ripley Springs. The company expected to create a large resort called Virginia Mineral Springs and built a bowling alley, a swimming pool, tennis courts and an open air dance pavillion. The automobile came of age in the 1920s, however, and changed summer vacation habits. The resort never met the expectations of the partners.

In 1925, W.T. Graham sold out to two men —Claiborne and Eades. But the depression ended all hopes for the resort business, and in 1931 the entire hotel burned down, probably at the hand of an arsonist.

Today there are private cottages on the site of the hotel, and the four springs of the old Ripley Springs are all overgrown.

Yellow Massanutten Springs

Located three miles east of Lacy Springs, Rockingham County. The resort was owned and operated by Mr. Charles Brock, who renamed his Brock's Springs, Yellow Massanutten Springs.

An 1876 brochure states that this resort was opened the year before with a large three-story hotel and cottage. It mentions also a bar and bowling alley and two bath houses with a shower and plunge bath. A carriage service was offered between the resort and Harrisonburg, 12 miles away. Five different types of water were found here, and physicians of the day maintained that this water offered a cure for "Cholera Infantum" or "Summer Complaint," which struck so many children in the cities during the summer. About the time of the First World War, all the buildings were razed.

There are dozens and dozens of other small resorts that have passed into oblivion. Some are known by name only, while others have left behind a record of the county in which they were located even though there is no record of when they flourished and when they ceased to exist. These names, at least, should be added to the annals of the histories of the two Virginias.

Craig County had Minadoka, Caldwell Healing, Craig Alum and Webbs Springs. Chalybeate and Mungel's Springs and Alum Wells were located in Washington County. Williams' White Sulphur or Duvall's and Pembroke Springs were in Frederick County. Berry Hill Lithia Springs was in Culpeper County, Colemen's Mineral Springs in Cumberland County and Jefferson Park Springs in Albemarle County.

Two exotically named spas were Forest Lodge Lithia Springs in Hanover County and Harris Anti-Dyspetic and Tonic Springs in Nottoway County.

The list goes on and on: Otterburn Lithia Springs, Amelia County; Buckingham White Sulphur Springs, Buckingham County; Clifton and Iron Hill Springs, Allegheny County; Hagan's Springs, Scott County; Valley View and Kern's Springs, Shenandoah County; Wayland Springs, Nottoway County; Tazewell Sulphur and Cedar Bluff Sulphur Springs, Tazewell County; and Sudley Springs, Bland County; Wytheville and Core Lithia Springs, Wythe County; Crystal Sulphur Springs, Augusta County; and in the county of Bath—so named for its many spas— Wallawhatoola Alum, Bolar, Panther and All Healing springs. All are lost and forgotten.

If these hills could only talk. . .

Grayson Sulphur Springs.

Millboro Springs from an old lithograph.

The ballroom of Blue Healing Springs is in poor but stable condition.

SHENANDOAH ALUM.

Main building and grounds of Shenandoah Alum Springs in 1883, from a B and O Railroad pamphlet. VA

THE SHANNONDALE SPRINGS.

Shannondale Springs on a peninsula of the Shenandoah River in 1845.   VA

FRONT VIEW OF HOTEL

Front view of the hotel at Variety Springs.

Mr. Wilbur Detamore
Staunton, Virginia

The hotel at Virginia Mineral Springs, moved from New Castle in 1912. It burned down in 1931. VA

THE ALUM SPRINGS.

WALLAWHATOOLA

ALUM AND CHALYBEATE

SPRINGS.

WM A. SITLINGTON, PROPRIETOR.

P. O. MILLBORO SPRINGS, BATH CO. VA.

Board per Day, $1.50
" Week, 10.00
" Month, 35.00
Children under 10 years of age and colored servants half price.

This water will be supplied in cases or demijohns.

PACKARD

The hotel at Black Rock Resort before the disastrous fire in 1909.   Robert P. Daughtry
Waynesboro, Virginia

Guests at Black Rock Resort around the turn of the century.   Robert P. Daughtry
Waynesboro, Virginia

The second Mercer Healing Springs Hotel, built in 1911-1912.

Michael Meador
Madison, W. Va.

The present dwelling at the site of Mercer Healing Springs is on the site of the old hotel, amid surviving outbuildings. To the left of the house is the hotel's former kitchen springhouse and the low building on the right once served as servant's quarters and laundry.

Michael Meador
Madison, W. Va.

The hotel at Cluster Springs also served as the home of the headmaster of the Cluster Springs Academy. One of the dormitories is in the left background. This building burned down in the 1930s.
Mrs. W.W. Williams
South Boston, VA

The Ryburn Cottage is the only original building still standing at Cluster Springs.
Mrs. W.W. Williams
South Boston, VA

Bibliography

Burke, William, **The Mineral Springs of Western Virginia with Remarks on Their Use**, 2nd. Ed., Wiley and Putnam, 1846.

Burke, William, **The Mineral Springs of Virginia**, Morris and Brother, 1851.

Crook, James K., **The Mineral Waters of the United States and Their Therapeutic Uses**, 1899.

Fishwick, Marshall, **Springlore in Virginia**, Popular Press, 1978.

Ingalls, Fay, **The Valley Road: The Story of Virginia Hot Springs**, World Publishing Co., 1949.

MacCorkle, W.A., **White Sulphur Springs**, 1916

Moorman, J.J. **The Virginia Springs**, J.B. Lippincott, 1859

Moorman, J.J., **Mineral Springs of North America**, J.B. Lippincott, 1873

Newbraugh, Frederick, **Warm Springs Echoes**, 3 vols., 1967-77

Pencil, Mark, **The White Sulphur Papers, or Life at the Springs of Western Virginia**, 1839

Pollard, Edward, **The Virginia Tourist**, J.B. Lippincott, 1870

Price, Paul, McCue, J.B., Hoskins, Hamer, **Springs of West Virginia**, W.Va. Geological Survey, 1936

Prolix, Peregrine, **Letters Descriptive of the Virginia Springs**, 1834 and 1836.

Many newspapers and magazine articles, archival pamphlets and unpublished manuscripts from libraries and historical societies in both states are also available for further reading.